Deares

Dès Masquerade:

An Exposé on Satan in The New Age Movement

Thank you for blessing me with wonderful loving words

Stay Blessed

Rev. Dr. Diana Hardy

By: Reverend Diana Hardy

Dès Masquerade: **An Exposé on Satan in The New Age Movement**
by Reverend Diana Hardy

ISBN # 0-89228-149-9

Copyright ©, 1999, by Reverend Diana Hardy

Published for the author by
Impact Christian Books, Inc.
332 Leffingwell Ave.,
Kirkwood, MO 63122
314-822-3309

Printed in the United States of America

Acknowledgements

I would like to take this opportunity to thank the people who helped me make this book a reality.

To My Executive Secretary, **Erica Johnson**, whose endless hours of editing, restructuring, sincerity, loving kindness and dedication has so inspired to bring out the best in me.

To The Treasurer, **Susannah Kuehnle**, a great mentee and dedicated student of the gospel of Jesus Christ whose generosity has made this book all the more possible.

Martha Buford Green, our Chairperson, who's advice came from heaven. We thank her for all the tender hours of dedication.

To **Reinaldo De Jesus** a great artist and confidant. Rey designed the cover of this book. He has displayed what true friendship is, always believing in my abilities and always being a great source of support. Rey, I bless the Name of the Lord for allowing the Lord to use you to bless me. I love you and you will always have a special place in my heart. Reino is the owner of RDJ Studios located in Brooklyn, NY.

The names of clients have been changed to protect their privacy. All Biblical quotes are from the *King James Version*, unless otherwise noted.

Dedication

I dedicate this book to my Father, Almighty God, whom I love passionately and who has inspired me to present this book to His people.

I love my Father for who He is and what He has been in my life.

He raised me, loved me, carried me, saved, me re-designed me, and when I was down and broken, He picked me up and fixed me.

Praise God for being God and for knowing how to take care of me when I didn't know how to take care of myself.

Oh praise Him, praise Him, praise Him. Glory Hallelujah!

Introduction

"Amazing Grace, how sweet the sound that
saved a wretch like me.
I once was lost but now I'm found."
(John Newton 1779)

The Holy Spirit guided every step involved in writing this book. I praise God for delivering me, and allowing me to share His infinite wisdom. The information contained in the following pages may offend many people but the truth has a way of doing that. Throughout our lives, we have unknowingly been deceived by lies and trickery disguised as answers to our everyday problems. We allow ourselves to be crippled by loneliness, despair, desperation, and fear; to fall prey to satan's tools of evil. But the truth lies in God. Here's where the blinders come off and the truth will look you straight in the face.

Whether you are reading this book because of some past, present or contemplated involvement in the dark arts, it is God's desire that you know the truth. He is going to reveal to you the lies that satan has fed you and that you have accepted. In accord with His Word, He is breaking Satan's stronghold on our minds. Glory to His Name!

CONTENTS

Chapter 1

Dès Masquerade

Kick off your shoes and get comfortable, it's nitty gritty time. The closet door is now being opened. Primarily, I want to address the ladies here. Although there are brothers who are participating in these practices, the ladies are approximately ninety percent of the targeted population. When I was "doing work" as they call it, I would work primarily on cases that were very difficult and out of the person's control, such as court cases that seemed stagnated or people who were harassing other people. But relationship cases were the biggy. Every other woman that came to me had a relationship problem. Whether they were married, dating or they wanting to date someone else's man, they all wanted relief from whatever relationship problem they were facing.

Most of the time it was the latter. You would be shocked to know the extremes to which women will go to get a man. Quite often, they have already put in their heads that they just have to have this man. They just know that even though he may be married or involved with someone else, he is the right person for them. Don't let them sleep with him! Once sex gets into the picture, it becomes all out war.

Usually, the men in these relationships tell women that their wives treat them badly. They eventually begin telling their wive's personal business. They will do their best to project themselves as loving husbands, and the victim in the relationship. So this becomes the woman's excuse for taking steps to end his relationship with his wife. She sells herself the lie that she is the better woman for him and sees the wife as the enemy. It isn't just older women or unattractive women who seek and utilize all kinds of witchcraft to get or keep a man. I've seen women from various socioeconomic backgrounds. Beautiful, intelligent women mired in insecurity seeking help with their relationships.

Oh! Excuse me! I guess some of you think that burning a candle and using his picture along with any personal items of his is just sweetening him up. Ladies, wake up and smell the desperation. Whether you do the above or similar practices, you are doing witchcraft. You are summoning demonic spirits to do your bidding. It is a foul sin and totally against the will of God. The Bible says: *There shall not be found among you any one that maketh his son or his daughter to pass through the fire, or that useth divination, or an observer of times, or an enchanter, or a witch, or a charmer, or a consulter with familiar spirits, or a wizard, or a necromancer.* (Deut 18:10-11).

The same Moses whom God spoke to on Mount Horeb, wrote these laws as the Father told them to him. I know you may well believe that was just for the Old

Testament. The Bible says that God never changes; His Word still stands. That Scripture means the same today as it did when Moses wrote it thousands of years ago.

In the New Age Movement, people are openly practicing divination, such as tarot cards, claiming to do spiritual readings from God. This is an illusion, a tool of Satan straight from hell. If you are one of those people receiving information from tarot cards, the Bible tells you plainly in black and white that this is not of God. (2 Kings 17:17). You are not receiving information from the Holy Spirit, you are getting your information from demons.

There are many forms of divination. For example runes is an old Celtic divination system heavily saturated in paganism and worship of strange gods. Runes are small rectangular stones that have various symbolic markings on them. To derive an answer from them one would ask the question and shake the runes stones together in a bag and then cast them onto a surface. The runes are read according to which pattern comes out. This would be the answer to your question. Communication with spirit guides has also become a very big part of the New Age. In the New Age philosophy, it is believed as well as taught by many that everyone was born with at least five spirit guides. These are spirit beings, who are supposedly helping you on your spiritual path, protecting you, as well as giving you psychic information about your life and others.

Another area that is widely accepted and practiced is

contacting angels for spiritual guidance. Workshops on contacting your guardian angel or other heavenly angels are conducted throughout North America. It is taught that God has given every one a guardian angel and that by prayer and meditation you can call upon that angel for assistance in times of need. Posters and statues of these angelic beings are being sold in many New Age shops. People are going so far as to name their angels. Relying upon any angelic hosts for assistance in any matter is a form of worship and is a sin. The Bible says: *Let no man beguile you of your reward in a voluntary humility and worshipping of angels, intruding into those things which he hath not seen, vainly puffed up by his fleshly mind.* (Colossians 2:18). Plainly, this Scripture is stating that anyone who promotes the propaganda that you can communicate with God's heavenly angels is speaking from made up thoughts.

This is an area where Satan has taken many opportunities to interfere with human beings. The Bible says: *no wonder, for Satan himself masquerades as an angel of light.* (2 Corinthians 11:14). Angel worship is another form of idolatry. We, as human beings, cannot command angels to perform special blessings for us. If, out of ignorance, you are an individual who feels that you are communicating with an angelic being, you have been duped. You are communicating with demons trying to pass themselves off as God's servants.

Although the Bible speaks of heavenly hosts (angels) visiting mankind, sometimes even in the fleshly form, this only occurs when Almighty God sends them as a messenger to you. Neither you nor I call upon the angels of the Lord at our convenience. It is troubling to me to know that people can take hold of an idea and claim it as gospel, as fact.

Past Life Regression is another popular practice. New Agers claim that through reincarnation, when we die, our soul comes back to continue to learn lessons. According to this philosophy, multiple lives are necessary for the evolution of our spirit. They also claim, once we have evolved high enough, we do not have to return to the physical world. As a result, people are running around looking for their soul mates, which is supposedly someone that they were closely connected to in another life. This is usually the theory used when we meet someone new, but it feels that we've known them before. Sometimes a person may feel an inexplicably strong connection or attraction to someone or experience an event that feels strongly familiar. The term déjà vu is attributed to reincarnation.

Practitioners use hypnosis as a medium for Past Life Regression which is supposed to enable the practitioner to regress the client back to previous lifetimes. Not only is there no concrete proof of anyone living other lives but the purpose and intent of past life regression is unclear even in theory. The Bible says: *And as it is appointed unto men one to die, but after this the judgment.* (Hebrews 9:27) (KJV).

This is ludicrous, this will thoroughly have you

13

believing a lie. Those of you who are participating in past life regression in any form, be it to gain information from a past or present life, you are being lied to. What happens to you when you are in a state of regression is that your mind has the ability to bring up images that can come from many places. The mind is a powerful vehicle. How many times have you visualized something in your mind or had a passing thought from out of nowhere?

Many psychologists are now engaging in an area commonly referred to as Regression including Past Life Regression. Regression is when the therapist induces a hypnotic state and regresses you back into your childhood. This treatment is usually used when there are problems that surface in the patient's life that are reoccurring. This type of therapy is used to bring the problem to surface so that the patient and doctor can both recognize it and begin to treat it. Past Life Regression is a theory that has been around for centuries but has become very strong in the last two decades. It is thought by practitioners and lay people alike that one's soul has lived more than once and if you go to the bookstores you will find books on Reincarnation and related themes.

People today are embracing this theory more and more. Past life regression is also induced while in a hypnotic state. The doctor or hypnotist supposedly takes the patient back in their mind into previous lives. Lives where they could have been anything such as a man, woman, an animal, royalty, or a slave from any culture. This is one of Satan's favorite and easily accessible areas of domination. We know that psychiatrist deal with mental disorders, which means their area of expertise is the <u>mind.</u> What better way to cause total chaos and possible severe mental problems then Satan gaining entrance and controlling the minds of God's people?

Satan works on us through our thoughts. He will have you thinking all kinds of things. As long as he can keep your mind off of seeking God, he can put all kinds of obstacles in your way. Sometimes he will bring about that very thing that you have desired for so long, especially if it is not good for you. He does not want you to start focusing on what God wants you to do. The Bible says that the Lord has a multitude of blessings for those that He loves. Without a doubt, the New Age Movement and all of its practices are tricks and tools of Satan. This New Age spirituality has no connection to the One True and Living God. Satan, the "god of this world," has deceived thousands upon thousands of people with this instant spirituality.

New Age principles are based on teachings that encourage you to get in touch with your inner self and that human beings can access any information that they want by doing so. It also teaches you to totally rely on yourself; the whole focus of this syndrome is for you to have control over every aspect of your life. The Word of God teaches us to *cast all of our cares onto the Lord, for He careth for us* (1Peter 5:7). Whenever we have a problem we are suppose to go to God about it. This is why it is very important that we seek the Lord while He

15

may be found.

As children of an Almighty Father, we need to establish a personal relationship with God and the only way to do that is through His Son our Lord and Savior Jesus Christ. Jesus said: "No man can come to the Father except by me." Sinners are not the only ones participating in this monstrosity, saints (Christians) are as well. Many pastors would be surprised how many female parishioners have come to me trying to solicit help in getting a man through witchcraft. I have been offered large sums of money for such cases but I have never indulged in that practice. To tie a man up in this manner only uses satanic beings that may hurt the man. These demons will try to attack the intended victim as well as cause a curse to fall upon me, my children and the person who paid me.

You'd be surprised to know how much money is paid to unethical people who do this kind of work, sometimes charging thousands of dollars. People who look for this type of work are operating under a spirit of desperation. Satan has twisted their thoughts and emotions so that he can eventually destroy them. As you read earlier, satan is a thief and a liar. If he can destroy you, believe me, he will. The New Age Movement was founded by satan to create a delusion that would take your focus off of the Living God. We are not independent of God; without Him we could not even wake up in the morning. It is only by His grace that we can even open our eyes each morning. When we are ill, it is His Word that commands our body to heal. Without Him, we are nothing.

We all must establish a relationship with Him through Jesus Christ, our Lord and Master, as He is the only One that can protect us from the *"devourer of the brethren."* We humans are spiritually dead because of the sin that Adam and Eve, our forefathers, committed in the Garden of Eden. The Bible says: *"That in the day that you eat thereof you shall surely die."* The Lord was speaking directly to Adam. The death that God was speaking about was a spiritual death. Even though Adam and Eve were suppose to live forever, through free will they committed a sin for which God said they would die. So it is through them that we are born into sin and therefore "spiritually dead."

But God provided another way for His people to have another chance at "eternal life." The Bible says: *For God so loved the world that He sent His only begotten Son, that whosoever believeth in Him shall not perish, but shall have everlasting life.* (John 3:16). Yes, the same Jesus Christ of Nazareth who died for you and me on Calvary's cross. So you see, when you accept Jesus Christ into your life as your Lord and Savior, at that moment you are regenerated, (made spiritually alive again). The Holy Spirit, who is the third Person of the Trinity, comes to dwell in you. All your sins are wiped clean and you become a new creature in Christ. For this reason we ought to lift up holy hands and praise God for His everlasting love and glorious Salvation. Many of us, if we are truthful with ourselves, know that we have done many horrible things to other people as well as ourselves. We are in need of a Savior.

Once you accept Jesus Christ as your Lord and Savior, you become an heir to the Throne of Grace. As Christians, we have so many wonderful privileges and blessings in store for us. As long as we are obedient and faithful to our Father's Word, He will guide us into all righteousness. When you think about all the wonderful promises you could have as a born again believer, why would you want to accept the scraps that Satan gives you? He is not faithful to those who do his bidding, he will take everything you have, your possessions, your money, your home, your children, your career, and when he's finished, he will try to take your life. He's a cheater who twists the truth for his own desires and is only out for himself.

You may ask, "Why would the devil want to destroy me?" That is a good question. The reason is because there is a war going on. Many are not aware, but there is a battle going on; we are in an all out war. The war I am talking about is a "spiritual" one. This is why counterfeit spirituality is on the rise. It's all part of the battle!

Satan cannot beat God; the only way to get back is by causing problems in the lives of God's children. We are God's favorite creation, and Satan knows that.

Why would you want to trade the blessings of a loving, generous and Almighty God for Satan's cursed offerings? In case you haven't heard it yet, Satan is a defeated foe. My Master, Jesus Christ, beat him at Calvary. He has no real power over you if you are a child of God (born again Christian). If you are serving the devil, you are on the wrong side, as my God is an Almighty God.

Don't continue to be deceived. If you are practicing the dark arts, using astrology or numerology or meditating on your higher consciousness, now is the time to stop. You may not want to take my word for it. Instead, pick up the Holy Bible, the living Word of God, and read it for yourself. If you still need proof, go to any Christian church that is without idols.

You are not to worship dead people whether they were saints or not, and that includes Mary. Just because she was the earthly Mother of Jesus does not mean that Mary can intercede for you or me; Mary is dead. Only one Man can intercede for you and me: Jesus Christ. He died, was resurrected and now is seated at the right hand of God, where He makes intercession for those who are His (Christians). The Bible says: *Neither is there salvation in any other: for there is none other name under heaven given among men, whereby we must be saved.* (The Acts 4:12) (KJV).

All kinds of New Age practitioner out there are advertising that they are healers, most with no prior medical knowledge and no knowledge of the anatomy but they make claims that the services they offer are a God given gift. This is what Jesus had to say about His disciples: *Heal the sick, cleanse the lepers, raise the dead, cast out devils: freely ye have received, freely give.* (Matthew 10:8).

When you are in service for the Lord, you are not to charge for laying hands on someone. God has given you this gift so that He can heal His people through you. I have witnessed and participated in a lot of these counterfeit healings. The practitioners charge anywhere from $50.00 -$200.00 per visit. There are no promises of recovery and generally, the client or patient feels very little if anything. Any gift that God has given is not to be used for monetary gain. You will often hear the practitioner say God gave them this gift, the Bible says different. Healing is from God and God alone. He is the giver of life and the sustainer of us all. He said, *But he was wounded for our transgressions, he was bruised for our iniquities: the chastisement of our peace was upon him; and with his stripes we are healed.* (Isaiah 53:5). Here the prophet Isaiah is talking about Jesus the Christ, the Son of God who died on Calvary. When He died, He took all our sins with Him. Jesus said that whatever we ask the Father in His Name we shall receive.

Now some of you may say that a doctor heals people. This is not so, the doctor treats the ailment either with a medical procedure or with medication for which he has received a strict training in medical science and human anatomy for years and is licensed before hanging out his shingle. Even then, he does not heal the person, God does. He is the One who commands the body to heal. Luke, who was one of the apostles, was a physician. He wrote one of the synoptic gospels as well as the Book of Acts. Nowhere in his writing do you find anybody channeling energy from the universe into someone's chakras or calling upon unknown entities to enlist them in healing a person.

Practitioners of the New Age arts will tell you that energy healing, Reiki, and chakra balancing are other forms of laying on hands healing in the Bible; however this is false. The Bible has this to say about laying on of hands: *"Lay hands suddenly on no man, neither be partaker of other men's sins keep thyself pure."* (1 Timothy 5:22). Instead, the Bible lets us know exactly where our healing comes from.

Long time therefore abode they speaking boldly in the Lord, which gave testimony unto the word of his grace, and granted signs and wonders to be done by their hands. (Acts 14:3)

Who forgiveth all thine iniquities; who healeth all thy diseases. Who redeemeth thy life from destruction; who crowneth thee with lovingkindness and tender mercies; Who satisfieth thy mouth with good things; so that thy youth is renewed like the eagles. (Psalms 103:3-5)

My son, attend to my words; incline thine ear unto my sayings. Let them not depart from thine eyes; keep them in the midst of thine heart. For they are life unto those that find them, and health to all their flesh. (Proverbs 4:20-22)

He healeth the broken in heart, and bindeth up their wounds. (Psalms 147:3).

The Lord of Glory said in the Great Commission: *They shall take up serpents; and if they drink any deadly thing, it shall not hurt them; they shall lay hands on the sick, and they shall recover" (Mark 16:18).*

Jesus also said that anything that you ask in His Name, *He shall do.* This means that whenever we pray, we ought to pray to the Father in the Name of Jesus. There is no such healing that calls for you to channel energy into someone's body. Chakra healings, channeling energy, Rieki, crystal healing and all of that type are counterfeit healing.

The colors of the rainbow are a topic that the New Age has recently shed much light on. The Bible talks about the significance of the rainbow in the book of Genesis chapter 9. God established the rainbow after the Flood as a reminder to Him that He made a covenant with mankind never to destroy the world by water again. Although this is God's meaning for the rainbow, the New Age has changed its meaning and significance. When you hear New Agers talk about the colors of the rainbow, they usually refer to the chakras, which are allegedly spiritual energy center that each human being has within his or her body. The chakras are said to work in conjunction with the glands. It is taught in the New Age that whatever physical or mental health problems we have are directly related to the chakra that deals with that area and can be corrected through changing the energy of the chakra as well as sending energy to heal it. Reiki and Chrakra polarity are just a few. There are even some medical doctors who are embracing these New Age therapies and encourage their patients to try them. Color Therapy, Reiki, and even Past life regression are among the treatments that are being offered by some physicians.

Counterfeit healing is a gray area to many who would just as soon not talk about it. There are many church-going folk who participate in this falsehood. We have established that all healing is from God. It is by His spoken Word that we are healed and when we are in need of healing, we are to go to the Father in prayer. The Bible says take everything to the Lord in prayer. It also says: *Cast all your cares upon the Him; for He careth for you.* (1 Peter 5:7)

Satan is a counterfeiter and a liar. The reason that Satan was kicked out of Heaven was because of his pride and his desire to be exalted above God. The book of Isaiah recounts it this way: *How art thou fallen from heaven, O Lucifer, son of the morning! How art thou cut down to the ground, which didst weaken the nations! For thou has said in thine heart, I will ascend into heaven, I will exalt my throne above the stars of*

23

God; I will sit also upon the mount of the congregation, in the sides of the north. I will ascend above the heights of the clouds; I will be like the most High. Yet thou shalt be brought down to hell, to the sides of the pit. (Isaiah14: 12-15)

Jesus said in the book of St. Luke Chapter 10 and verse 18th: *I beheld Satan as lightning fall from heaven.* Here we see that Satan was cast out of heaven and ever since then he has been in rebellion against God and his people. Satan's fate has already been sealed, he has already been judged. What he wants to do is take every one of God's people with him into the pits of hell. He knows that you are God's favorite creation and that he is hated, so he is literally trying to destroy you. Whether it is physically or emotionally, he doesn't care, he will take you any which way he can. Satan has conjured up all kinds of devices and theory and practices to get you caught up into a continuously sinful life. A life that will cut you off from God.

Counterfeit gifts are Satan's area of expertise. Since Satan could not exalt himself above God, he is always searching for a way to accomplish his goals through God's people. In the Kingdom of God, the Lord established spiritual gifts which operate by way of His precious Holy Spirit. In 1 Corinthian chapter 12, the apostle Paul speaks about the nine gifts of the Spirit, listed below.

> *word of wisdom*
> *word of knowledge*

faith
gifts of healing
working of miracles
prophecy
discerning of spirits
divers kinds of tongues
interpretation of tongues

All are from the same Spirit. These are only for the Body of Christ, which are born again Christians. They are given to us for many reasons, including edification, comfort, teaching etc. They are not given to individuals who are not of the Body of Christ (Christians). The gifts enable us to do many things for God's people and God has given a gift to every one of His people.

Satan knows this and has caused much confusion in this area. He has concocted counterfeit gifts that are to manifest like the "gifts" of God but there are distinctions. Satan's gifts are:

1. false wisdom
2. false knowledge
3. lack of faith in God & faith in his devices
4. false healing techniques such as: Reiki, energy channeling, polarity, psychic surgery, etc.
5. manipulating miracles
6. false prophecy
7. false discerning of spirits
8. satanic tongues
9. lying interpretations

Who are Satan's soldiers?...psychics, mediums, spiritualists, channelers, healers that perform "healing" as mentioned above, transchannelers, shamans, astrologers, numerologists, persons who participate in Santeria, anyone who communicates with spirit guides, or ascended masters, reincarnation, karma, past life regression therapy, runes, tarot, palmistry, eye readings, tea leaves, voodoo, etc.

The information that these people receive is given to extort money from you. Even when they give you information that appears to be true, there is always a reason why Satan gives information: to get you hooked so that you will become dependent on him for information. He is very well disguised, he uses psychics who profess they believe in God. Well, even Satan believes in God and can quote the Scriptures verbatim. Once you start going to psychics and receiving information that actually happens, you start to depend on them and even refer friends and family to them. You are now worshipping Satan on a regular basis; you have given him what he has desired for so long, all the attention. Your focus has turned from God. This is dangerous because Satan does not love you; he will use you, abuse you, and if he can, destroy you. Instead, turn your focus to Almighty God, for He is the One who has put the breath of life into you. He wakes you up every morning and starts you on your way. He brings the entire family blessings, financial blessings, and protection from dangers, love and good health to you.

Do not accept the monetary strings attached to the devil's deed when you can be blessed beyond your every thought and when its all over inherit Eternal Life, something that Satan will never have. He is going to be destroyed. See Revelation 20:10 but don't just read verse 10, read all of it and see his final demise.

I'm sure that you don't want to be caught up in that situation with him. You may be a person who is involved in these types of works and wants to get out and Satan may be telling you that God will never forgive you or accept you. Well the devil is a liar. God said repent, and confess your sins to Him and except Jesus Christ as your Lord and Savior. It is for this very reason that Jesus died on the Cross at Calvary, to disarm the forces of darkness and to deliver His people out of the bondage of Satan and bring them into the Light giving to them Eternal Life. Why not free yourself this day, this moment. God is waiting for you, all you have to do is get on your knees and tell God that you are sorry for any participation in these areas. Ask the Lord Jesus to come into you life and change it. Renounce Satan and all his cohorts, tell him it's over and you will never again serve him. Ask God to show you the Truth, for when you do this, you will have crossed over from death into Eternal life.

Chapter 2

Passions Under Seige

Women, I would like to dedicate this chapter to you. We like to think we are in control of our intimate relationships with the opposite sex and this may be true to a certain degree. When a woman meets a man that she has an instant attraction to, she begins her mission to find out about his life. In this way she will assess what she is up against, or if this person is even worth pursuing. Once she determines what his situation is, and ladies, you know we have our ways of finding out what we want to know. If he still seems desirable, then the chase is on.

If she determines that her attraction to this man is strong enough, her emotions may begin to override some of the red flags that shoot up early in the relationship which indicate she should <u>not get</u> involved any further with this man. Women go to different extremes to "catch" the man that they want. When their personality, femininity and beauty do not work, they try other options. I have had many women approach me asking if magic or voodoo would help them get the man they want.

When I was a New Age practitioner, I counseled hundreds of people from diverse backgrounds. Primarily, women sought out my services. I have evidenced much suffering in my own personal life because of some of the decisions. As a result of my making sacrifices and offering to the orishas (gods in Ifa), I've experienced difficulties in various areas of my life. At the time of my involvement in Ifa, many of the doors that were usually opened to me closed. The more that these false deities do for you, the more you have to give them.

Usually, when a woman decides she wants a man, she will do almost anything to get him. She's willing to do things she knows are wrong.

Self-esteem is a major factor in relationships. It dictates whether you demand respect from someone on all levels or whether you are willing to allow them to do just about anything their little heart desires. The first thing a woman uses is her feminine charms. A man will know almost immediately after entering into a conversation with a woman in what regard she holds herself. Not only does he note your conversation, but your demeanor and body language as well. Don't be fooled young ladies, men are not as naive as you think. Ladies, we need to seriously work on ourselves. First we need to establish a strong relationship with our Heavenly Father, through His Son, Jesus Christ who came in the flesh. When we accept Him and bond with Him, we may begin to ask Him to change us into the women that He wants us to be.

Whatever we gain in life, whether it be knowledge, love, financial wealth, joy, it should all come from Him and nowhere else. Because if it comes by any other means, it will have attachments to it that can spell disaster.

Often when we get into relationships, our emotions come under seige. I like to call it *passions under siege*. We start off feeling in control of ourselves, but as soon as we feel we're in love, things began to shift. Everything is all right until the man displays some facet of his personality that's always been there, but we refused to acknowledge, because we were in love with the illusion.

Once we have a man in our life, many of us will go to any extreme to keep him. We could talk about all of our fears, hurts, and needs, but that is another book. Right now, I want to focus on some of the lengths you ladies will go to get a man. I have encountered many women who are in long term relationships, be it marriage or just *"my man"* relationships. They have made such requests as having something done to keep their husbands/boyfriends from moving or contemplating divorce. The all time "biggie" is somehow eliminating the other woman.

The questions would start. "Does he love her? How did they meet? Is he having sex with her?" And so on. It seems as thought we hate ourselves so much that we torture ourselves with such information. Ladies, look where we have gone in our pursuit of an honest, loving relationship. We have the wrong focus. We need to put our focus on God. He will provide all of our needs. If it is a relationship that you desire, the best and only choice should be with a man that God sends to you.

God does not condone intimate sexual relationships outside of marriage, so if you are praying to God and asking him to let you have a man who is married, know God does not put His hands in anything like that. You can run around lusting all you want. It will get you into nothing but trouble. I have counseled women who tolerate so much abuse from a man because they are scared to lose him. Many of us seem to think that our sexual organs have special glue. That a man they are having difficulty holding onto will never leave, if they sleep with him. Well, if you ladies believe that, you are in for a rude awakening.

It is time that we get ourselves together. Stop utilizing psychics, paying large sums of money to get a man, or help keep a man. Remember when a psychic or spiritualist does any kind of work for you, they are enlisting the aid of demonic spirits. This now opens you or your children to all kinds of demonic disturbances affecting every aspect of your life and your children's lives. Even if it works, it will only work for a little while. This kind of work destroys relationships, ending them in hatred and resentment. There is hell to pay for everyone involved.

Satan will make you pay and not only with money. You cannot <u>make</u> someone love you or want you, if they do not. There is no form of magic that can do this. Remember Almighty God is still in control. You are forcing your will upon someone else. Almighty God gave us free will. We have no right to try to control other people. Practitioners of this type of work are <u>not serving</u> God, they are serving Satan. You are serving Satan when you are having this kind of work done. God's wrath will come upon you. Do not be fooled. If you have to go to resort to these tactics then whatever it is you want is not meant for you. Also, consider the severity of destroying something so sacred as marriage. Some of you have no guilt or remorse. Jesus said: (regarding marriage) *What therefore God have joined together let no man put asunder.* (Matthew 19:6) (KJV).

Understand that when you perform these kinds of actions, you are sending a demon to hurt another woman. Satan will not just stop at tearing apart the relationship; he will perform many other brutal acts. Remember he can only do what God allows him to do. Don't be a willing assistant, a partner to his torturous, life-threatening acts. Satan is feeding you a lie, an illusion–*Dès masquerade.* He will rob you of everything you have and, if possible, take your life. As children of an Almighty God, who is worthy of all of our love, trust, and commitment, we could have better health, love, family life, supernatural power, and protection if we would heed God's Word, which is the Bible. If we would rely on God daily to give us our provisions, we would have a better quality of life. We need to ask God to teach us patience. The Bible has this to say about patience:

Wait on the Lord: be of good courage, and he shall strengthen thine heart: wait, I say, on the Lord. (Psalms 27:14)

I waited patiently for the Lord; and he inclined unto me, and heard my cry. *(Psalms 40:1)*

Here is the patience of the saints; here are they that keep the commandments of God, and the faith of Jesus. *(Revelation 14:12)*

An impatient, emotional, and discouraged person is an open playground for Satan's foul play. This is why it is extremely important that we keep our focus on God, making sure that we learn the Word of God. We must know it for ourselves, in order that no man may be able to tell us to do or believe things that are not pertaining to Almighty God.

Chapter 3

Generational Sins

Early childhood is an amazing time in our lives. We are so innocent and impressionable. We look to our parents and family for our basic needs. In fact, most of our information about the world comes from them. I remember growing up (in the projects) with my family. My dad worked every day, and when he came home, he'd sit in the kitchen where he'd pick up some tidbits of what had gone on in the house that day. He was always conveniently kept in the dark, at my mother's request. My mom stayed home with us four kids. For her, being a mother was a full time job; she didn't feel the need for a job outside of home.

My mom loved to play the numbers and still does even today. Like most people who play numbers, she was always looking for something that would bring good luck. She had horseshoes, rabbits' feet; she'd even throw pennies around the house and burn lucky incense. These things were a part of our everyday lives. She used them to bring her luck playing numbers. Although these things never worked, she continued to believe in them. Some of her friends with the same vice would always encourage her participation.

One day a lady introduced my mother to the *Seven*

African Powers candle for luck. Even though she didn't know who they were, she went out and bought the candle along with some *Seven African Powers* incense. She used them at least once a week. This new ritual went on for quite a while. Since I was only about nine years old at the time, I really did not pay much attention to any of this. Oddly enough, it was here that my entrapment began. What my Mother had done out of ignorance would later cause the entire household great confusion and agony in years to come.

My dad was a fairly passive person; a man who usually kept to himself. He did not subscribe to, nor approve of, my mother's practices. My father had accepted Jesus Christ as his Lord and Savior. Like many other spouses, he did not want to cause an argument, so he did not say much about it. Besides, my Mother had a way about her. She would voice her desires and opinions with force and resonance. Hence, she usually got her way.

In hindsight, it saddens me to know that as a parent, as an adult <u>Christian,</u> my dad allowed us to become susceptible to such blatant idolatry. Allowing a multitude of sins to infest our household. Unfortunately, this is old, familiar territory for those of us who come from a home where one parent knows the truth, believes Jesus is Lord, yet condones contrary practices such as burning candles, worshipping saints, and offering sacrificial incense for the purpose of calling up spirits to assist in obtaining their wants and desires. These practices provide Satan the opportunity to wreak havoc in the lives of the participants and all those around them.

While most of you may think that these kinds of practices cannot hurt the person practicing it or innocent bystanders who reside in the same house (children, other loved ones), it always does. Not only does this set up a destructive foundation but also opens the door for Satan and all his cohorts to enter and wreck havoc in their lives. As a direct effect, I, as well as other family members, became heavily involved in idolatry, witchraft, worshipping saints, orishas and Native American and African religions, both of which are often based on idolatry.

The susceptibility did not only lie with my parents. A neighbor downstairs in our building would have parties for a highly recognized saint among some Hispanics. At these parties, they would offer <u>sacrifices</u> of food, wine, money, and prayers in return for success in their lives. My mother would send me to these parties to get plates of food to bring home. Although I did not pay much attention to everything that was going on, nor did I know the deities' name, I remember exactly what the saint looked like.

Years later, I became deeply involved in worshiping this deity. I want you to know that my involvement in this form of idolatry was not coincidental. I was branded (set up by the enemy), ushered into a ceremony with a demonic being who would claim me. What my Mother unknowingly created was an opportunity for spiritual bondage. She willingly sent her young, innocent daughter into a den of demons.

This all happened because my mom wanted to taste my neighbors' cooking and she probably was not even aware of the multitude of sins that she would put upon my shoulders. I will not speak of my other siblings' bondages. I will simply say that they encountered many subsequent problems as well.

Let me interject here that what we say and do as parents WILL and DOES affect our children. The Word of God says the *'curse fell upon us,'* and Satan found just the right opportunity to take advantage of that situation. Jesus told His disciples, *The thief cometh not but for to steal and to kill and to destroy. I come that they may have life and that they may have it more abundantly.* (John 10:10) Sin is the open door for generational curses, the open door for all curses. The sins of the parents can and will affect the child.

Candle burning is becoming a common, everyday practice in many households. Christians and nonbelievers alike, participate in this sinful practice. One of the major problems with people today is a lack of patience. People get trapped into get rich quick schemes and dreams of overnight success, because they're out for instant gratification. Many of us forget that Almighty God supplies all our needs from birth and that it is only at His command that we accomplish anything in life. We must wake up and recognize the wonderful and Sovereign Father we have. We should give honor and praise to Him daily for His generous blessings. I don't know anyone who can say that God has not blessed them. Many people, out of ignorance, burn candles because they don't want to work in God's time frame. We've all felt the frustration of wondering when He's going to give us what we want. If we all were truly honest with ourselves, most of us would have to admit that we have participated in some form of dark art at some point in our lives.

Whether it is burning candles, setting a white elephant behind the front door, purchasing a Buddha statue, carrying rabbits' feet, or placing horse shoes over the door, these practices as well as many others are an abomination to Almighty God. The Lord says, *Thou shalt not bow down thyself unto them, nor serve them: for I, the Lord thy God, am a jealous God, visiting the iniquity of the Fathers upon the children unto the third and fourth generation of those who hate me.* (Deuteronomy 5:9)

Chapter 4

Effects of Generational Sins

In today's society, even believers are seeking "instant spirituality." They want the quick fix. Hence, the New Age Movement began. The New Age syndrome is playing a major role in spirituality today. People have turned from conventional religion to the many facets of New Age "Religion." Just about every learning center in America offers seminars and lecturers on how to utilize the earth's energy force. "Healing energy" has become a well-known term. People of all ages are getting involved, from young children to senior citizens. Everywhere people are buying books and pamphlets on how to develop psychic abilities, work with Chakras (energy centers located throughout the human body that correspond to specific glands), reiki, trance Channeling, transcendental meditation, healing wands, contacting spirit guides, and working with angels. Even Native American traditions are increasing in popularity among believers and non-believers.

In the metaphysical world, I became a well-known, and respected practitioner. I taught classes on spiritual development, working with the Chakras, crystals, spirit guides, etc. I quickly discovered that many New Age people who are looking for an extra income became teachers, lecturers, and healers overnight. Very often they have no formal or structured educational training. Usually, their information was obtained either by attending seminars that someone else was teaching, or by reading several books on the subject. Students of New Age practices can quickly become teachers, teachers that charge fees for their services.

Reiki is one of the most popular teachings available today. It is amazing that anyone can take Reiki-Level 1, 2, and 3 seminars, and with no, or very little, knowledge of the human anatomy, can hang out a shingle as a professional Reiki healer. In these three levels, someone called a master reiki healer teaches the student. This is a person who probably paid about nine hundred dollars and spent 12 hours in instruction to learn how to utilize the Reiki technique. The teaching consists of a total of nine hours spread over a few months, and after nine hours of instruction, they are called a master.

Reiki is based on the principle of energy transference into the spiritual bodies via the chakras. Generally, this type of energy manipulation, which takes place between the practitioner and the client, is supposed to clear energy blockages and strengthen and accelerate healing in various organs of the body.

What is not taught is that this is an illusion of Satan. He has devised this system to ensnare God's people. When a person applies Reiki to you, many things can come into play. Once you have consented to treatment the practitioner lays you down on a flat surface and asks you to remove any clothing articles that might be a hindrance to the energy passing through your system. Next, the practitioner uses different hand positions over your whole body, thus allowing her body (the practitioner's) to become an open channel for the transference of energy into your body. If you are concerned about different unwanted energies, such as spirits of an unknown origin or realm, passing through your body and voice your concern to the practitioner, she/he will usually tell you that they have put a field of protective white light around you and that absolutely <u>no harm</u> will come to you.

This is absolutely unfounded and untrue. As a former New Age practitioner, I had the opportunity to witness and counsel many people who have been involved in this kind of work as well as other New Age practices. I can recall instances when people suddenly experienced bouts of depression, insomnia, outbursts of anger, and spirit communication after engaging in New Age practices. The process actually opens you up to receive unclean spirits. There is no healing involved here.

Another widely accepted form of healing is crystal healing. Crystal healing has become very popular in the 1990's. There are many practitioners who utilize crystals for healing all types of physical ailments (e.g. high blood pressure, diabetes, metabolic problems, nervous system disorders etc). The retail prices of crystals range from fifty cents to hundreds of dollars. It is taught that crystals can be used in configuration or individually to work on the area of illness. This type of healing was quickly embraced due to the simplicity and inexpensiveness of the crystals.

Before I became involved in the New Age Movement, my background was in Christianity. Both my Mother and Father often talked to me about God and told me that Jesus Christ was the Son of God. Today, I bless the Name of the Lord; I have gained such an awesome and wonderful feeling of love for Him. I truly know that God is my anchor and I am His chosen vessel. To know that He has always had my life in His hands gives me such overwhelming comfort. Even when I was in error about His Word, I would always pray, asking Him to reveal the truth to me.

I am happy to say that God answered my prayers, He taught me through His Holy Spirit the truth about the many questions that I prayed about. I know that some of you may be saying right now, "Why hasn't He answered my questions pertaining to my life?" God will answer your questions, when you believe in your heart that He will answer them. Jesus said: *Ask, and it shall begiven you; seek, and ye shall find; knock, and it shall be opened to you.* (Luke 11-9) (KJV)

Although I didn't really understand who God was at my tender young age, I loved Him nevertheless. And today, with certainty, I know that He remains in my heart. As the tears fall down my cheeks at this moment, I thank Him for His unfailing love. Sincerely, I would not know who or where I would be right now if He hadn't delivered me from the snares of Satan. Like many other Christians and unbelievers, I fell for the same deceptive ideologies that Satan puts before us.

Throughout the time I participated in this New Age syndrome, I was consistent in my prayers, asking the Lord to show me if I was not serving or worshipping Him in the manner that He wanted me to.

It wasn't only the Metaphysical that I was involved in. I became involved in an offset of an African religion called Santeria. You know, the "get back to my roots," "it's a black thing," thing. Santeria is a combination of Catholicism and Ifa. Although I never participated in any of the initiations, praise God, I did set up altars and statues and made sacrifices to some of the deities. Santeria is a paganistic, demonic religion based on ancestral and deity worship. I realized the saint that I had seen in the lady's house when I was younger was now the same saint that I was offering sacrifices to. Recently, I asked the Holy Spirit why had I become involved with that religion and He gave me a vivid vision of a time when I was young. I saw my Mother burning a Seven African Powers candle (as I mentioned earlier, the sins of the forefathers....). The Ifa religion was introduced to me by a couple I consulted for a reading. The Ifa religion's core is the Seven African Powers. Generational curses are an area where there are gross misunderstandings, even among those who are in Christ. However the Bible speaks very clearly on this subject, and even gives us some examples of how curses can operate in our lives. Whether you are a believer or not, God's Word is true and if you live a life of sin, you will bring curses into your life as well as the lives of your future generations. In the story of Noah, who God commissioned to build the Ark, we meet his sons Shem, Japheth and Ham. The Bible says that Noah had a vineyard and one-day after partaking of the fruit of the vine, Noah, who was naked, fell into a drunken sleep. While he was sleeping, Noah's son Ham looked upon his father's nakedness. When Noah awakened from his sleep, he realized what Ham had done but did not curse Ham his son. Noah instead cursed Ham's son Canaan, saying: *Cursed be Canaan; a servant of servants shall he be unto his brethren.* (Genesis 9:25).

When God does something, He does it through the blood, be it curses or blessings. Your sins, or your righteousness can affect you, as well as your future generations. For this reason there are many problems that exist in families today that are the direct result of what our ancestors of yesterday have done. Often times, "dysfunctional" families are really cursed families. Not only are there generational curses on families but countries as well. Many catastrophic conditions such as illness and daily hardship are the result of generational curses stemming from past sins. Pagan worship has brought curses upon many. In the Old Testament, God told the Israelites not to intermarry with the outside nations they conquered because many of these countries practiced idolatry & paganism. The Israelites are God's chosen people through a covenant made with Abraham, the father of the Israelites (Genesis 15). God knew that if they married into those nations, that they would worship other deities, which is an abomination unto Almighty God. As a result God brought all manner of plagues and suffering upon them and it is the same for God's people today. Satan, knowing the Word of God, looks for an opportunity to bring misfortune into our lives; he knows that God said if you sin, these things will befall you. The Bible tell us, as born again Christians who have been redeemed, if we sin, we must confess our sins and repent before our Father.

We have an intercessor (Jesus Christ) who pleads on our behalf before the Father who wipes our sins away. However if we don't confess and repent of our sins right away, this gives grounds to Satan to go before the Throne of Grace to petition God to bring chaos into our lives. We must remember Satan is on the prowl, seeking whom he may devour. Poverty is a condition that is rampart in third world countries as well as in our society. Although we know what poverty is, there are many gross misconceptions as to how it occurs. I will focus on the spiritual reasons of this condition for the purposes set forth in this chapter. An example would be a family of financially poor individuals who from generation to generation live a life of poverty, passing it on from the adults to the children to the children's children and so on.

The Lord warns His people in the book of Deuteronomy, Chapter 28 about the blessings and the curses that would take hold on their lives according to whether they were disobedient or obedient. These same blessings and cursing are still in full force for God's people today. I recommend that you read Deuteronomy 28 for a more thorough understanding of God's blessings and curses.

Now I know that there are many of you who would argue the point that this is the Old Testament, but the Lord Jesus Christ said: *For verily I say unto you, Till heaven and earth pass, one jot or one tittle shall in no wise pass from the law, till all be fulfilled.* (Matthew 5:18) Just because you do not believe it does not mean that it is not so.

When we look around and see people who are homeless, living in the streets, people who cannot pay their rent, or who have difficulties putting food on the table, these conditions are curses. Even people who have ample incomes but cannot seem to keep any money and are always having to borrow to make ends meet are cursed. Another area where the effects of curses hinder God's people is genetic illnesses such as eczema, asthma, mental retardation, etc. These are all products of family curses.

Sickness is not from God. All manners of sickness, despair, depression, low self-esteem, etc., come from Satan. Illness comes about through sin and quite often many are paying for the past sins of our forefathers. You may be thinking, "Why does a child who is innocent come into the world mentally retarded or as a severe asthmatic who has to be consistently hospitalized?" The answer most often is found in generational curses. God said that if you sin, you would bring a curse upon yourself and your future generations. Now this is not to say that every descendent will be affected, some may not, but when you have many family members being plagued with the same diseases, then we can say with certainty that there is a curse operating in that family. A good example is families where someone has died of a heart attack in every generation. Medical science calls it genes; God calls it a curse. When you go to the doctor, he questions you about your family medical history. Doctors know that your family medical ailments or diseases could very well become a medical problem for you. Family medical history is one of the ways that insurance companies make determinations about health or life insurance.

I thank God that there is a way to be forgiven of all past sins and lay hold onto eternal life. In my extensive studies, it was revealed to me that when we encounter hardships in our lives for which there seems no apparent answer, our first recourse should be to take it to God in prayer and seek an answer as to why this curse is operating in our life. Let the Holy Spirit reveal to you any present or past sins of you family. Once He reveals it to you, then you should take steps for repentance and forgiveness for your family members both past and present. Ultimately, it is God who heals us and saves us from all adverse effects of these curses.

Sexual deviations such as pedophilia, incest, and

rape are by-products of curses upon the person performing these types of acts. Psychology has all kinds of theories for why a young man or woman would commit such acts. Although there are many theories, the bottom line is that it stems from spiritual conditions that often come through the lineage of that particular person. It would give greater understanding of a particular chaotic situation if we could investigate that person's family history, which often reveals why the curse is operating.

Sexual promiscuity, fornication and adultery are good examples of sins that lead to curses in an individual's life. Let's take a look at the story of King David. God said that David was a man after His own heart. However, David's sinful, adulterous acts with Bathsheba lead to her becoming pregnant with David's child. Bathsheba was married to one of King David's soldiers, Uriah, who was out in battle when the adulterous relationship took place. When David got word that Bathsheba was pregnant, he sent for Uriah and tried to get him to go home and sleep with his wife so that David would be able to cover up his sin. But when David's schemes did not work, he put Uriah on the front line of the battle so that he would be killed. David then took Bathsheba as his wife, but God informed David that the baby would not live because of the sinful acts that had been committed. Not only did David lose a newborn baby but also his other children's lives were severely affected by David's sin. One of his sons raped his daughter, and another brother, who found out what he

Dès Masquerade

did, killed him and then fled for his life. There were many curses that fell upon David's house because of his sins.

Demonic interference is a key area of interest for God's believers.Many Christians have little or no education about Satan or how his kingdom operates, which I will discuss later in chapter 5. Although demonic interference takes on several forms, I want to focus primarily on demons that pass from generation to generation. For example, a demon of drug abuse who moves from a parent onto their child. Demons familiarize themselves with your family; they are called "familiar" spirits because they know of conversations and things that were done before you were born. Some demons have a legal right to create havoc in your life due to a present day curse that is in effect upon your family.

For those of you whose families are plagued by curses of past or present sins, deliverance is needed as well as confession and repentance for the original sin that brought the curse about. If you feel that demonic activity has become a part of your everyday life, you should first take it to God in prayer, after which you should ask the Holy Spirit to direct you to a ministry which has an anointing for deliverance. Most deliverance churches can give you some direction on the matter. God is willing and able to deliver His people out of the bondage of Satan, but first we must seek God's face and renounce all of our connections to Satan and accept Jesus Christ as our Lord and Savior.

Depression is another emotional state of great concern to me. Mental health professionals have injected the drug Prozac into our society, like candy in a candy store. There are many people who are being told they have to take Prozac in order to function. If their partners leave them or they are stress out because of their work environment, psychiatrist now prescribing Prozac. Any kind of drug you take alters various chemical reactions in your body drugs, actually alter chemical reactions in your <u>brain.</u> Depression is a spirit that is sent by Satan to cause all kinds of emotional disturbances in your mind. Even though the doctors say there's a chemical imbalance, Satan still causes it. By becoming dependent (mentally and or physically) on a drug that actually alters the chemistry of your brain just to permit it to function, you play right into the hands of Satan and his demons. This will open up other opportunities to create psychological problems, which bring other treatments. Human beings most often are very impatient, but patience is something that Satan has a lot of. He will wait for the right opportunity to bring chaos into your life and just the right opportunity to try to destroy you, if he can.

Know that whatever ails you, you must take to God in prayer and believe that God will heal your problems. The Bible says that we can do all things through Christ who strengthens us. We don't need Prozac, we need Christ in our lives; we need to establish a personal relationship with Him where we take every thought to Him and it is Him whom we ask for strength, guidance, direction and love. So that when that man or woman leaves you for another, you will not fall apart. Not if you have Jesus Christ as your center. If you take hold of your Savior, He will keep you through the storms of life.

Chapter 5

Sisters and Brothers in Christ

Yes, I am speaking to the Christians who have come through my door; to all the Christians who are committing idolatry behind closed doors. If you are participating in these kinds of practices, my friend, you need deliverance. If you don't know that this is Satan worship, an abomination against the Lord God, you are now hearing from someone who used to embrace it. I beg of you to lift up your hands to the Almighty Father, confess your sins of idolatry and demon worship. Ask the Lord to forgive you for not trusting in Him and repent of all of your sins.

If you are afraid, empty out your heart to the Father. He did not give us a spirit of fear but a spirit of power, love and sound mind (2 Timothy 1:7). Prostrate yourself before God. He will take away the fear. Fear is nothing but a tool of the devil. Satan will try every low down, dirty trick in the book to hold you as his captive; he has blinded you to the truth. When you come to the Father in the Name of Jesus Christ of Nazareth, He will free you. The Bible says *If the Son of man therefore shall make you free, ye shall be free indeed.* (John 8:36). Why not stand on the Word of God? Glory to His precious Name. You may not be delivered overnight, but if you stay consistent in prayer and believe that God will deliver you, He will.

As born again Christians, we are afforded many opportunities that non-Christians do not share. We praise God because He is our Redeemer, our Comforter and our Strengthener. He loved us enough to <u>draw us to be a part</u> of His high calling. We are saved and santicified. We have been liberated from a multitude of sins and as the Holy Spirit works in our lives, we are to work toward becoming more like Christ.

Christians that read their Bibles, and attend church services are no strangers to Satan's tricks. However, with life's daily struggles, our faith is tested daily. Some of us have petitioned the Lord for things that we feel are a long time coming and in our haste and lack of faith we may allow the tempter to snare us with his deceptions. Although we lift up our "holy hands" on Sunday and praise the Lord, there are some of us who go home and immediately call the psychic lines requesting information as to whether we are going to receive that thing that we asked of the Lord. The Bible tells us to watch as well as pray. It amazes me that some Christians are still buying the Daily News just to read the horoscopes, to see if it applies to their situation for the day. Often you will hear others Christians tell people that they should not get involved in astrology and numerology but they themselves do not practice what they preach. Sisters and brothers, God is calling you to account for your sins.

We are living in the last and evil days, Christ is

coming for His church. We must prepare ourselves. As children of an Almighty Father, we serve a God who is Omnipresent, Omnipotent, and Omniscient. Anything that we desire or need to know we can ask of our Father for there is none greater than Him. Stop allowing Satan to deceive you by falling for his counterfeit information. In this world you are either a child of God or a child of Satan. If you are serving Satan, he won't bother you; the moment you decide to serve God and become born again, you will come under attack. You have become Satan's enemy; he will try to make your life miserable. However, as Christians, we don't have to worry, Jesus has equipped us with everything that we need to fight Satan. When we use our spiritual weapons in the Name of Jesus, we will have victory. Jesus said: ***Behold, I give unto you power to tread on serpents and scorpions, and over all the power of the enemy: and nothing shall by any means hurt you.*** (Luke 10:19)

You don't have to run, duck and hide; greater is He that is in us, than he that is in the world. Our fleshly or carnal nature has brought about actions on our part that have caused many peoples' lives to be in a state of constant turmoil. Human beings naturally desire to have a mate. After all, God instilled that desire in us. The Bible says that He gave Eve to Adam and commanded them to be fruitful and multiply. Women and men do desire one another. The problem arises when we view the opposite sex with our fleshly or carnal minds. We often enter into imitate relationships with preconceived ideas of a fairy tale relationship. By the end, we often come out confused and hurt because of our distorted views.

One of the most common problems with not waiting on God to send your mate, is that you then choose the wrong mate which takes you through a battlefield of arguments, disagreement, infidelity and often verbal or physical abuse. Satan has caused many of God's people to have a flesh connection whereby the FLESH produces most of their thoughts. They begin to desire relationships that display all the warning signs early in the relationship, sexual fantasies about their associates or friends' mate. Even to the point where they begin pursuing people who have a significant other. Satan knows that cross gender relationships are very important to mankind, so he will do everything that he can to keep your mind on the flesh and off of God. Women have solicited the services of spiritualists or psychics based on premature emotions about a man who they're either in a relation-ship with, or desire to be. They quite often will pray and ask God for the right mate to come into their lives, but when God takes too long for them, they go out and ask the devil to bring that man to them right away. That is just what you are doing when you go to any medium, psychic, spiritualist or anyone who is practicing magic to get that man. I've encountered people who have told me that burning a candle to St.Martin or St. Barbara is not magic. They do it in the Catholic Church; my mother has been burning candles all her life. This is their rationale, but God says different. God says that this is idol worship, which means that you, or the participant are actually worshipping the devil. I know that this statement may seem a little radical, but I've come to tell you the truth about Satan. He uses your flesh to deceive you and bring your emotions under seige; thinking that there's something wrong with yourself, because you don't have a mate. The devil is a lair!

We often enter into intimate relationships based our emotional needs at the time, which usually gives us the rose colored glasses effect that causes us to make the wrong choices in our selection of a mate. Many saints are being deceived in this area. We are allowing our emotions and loneliness to cloud our decisions. As saints in Christ and particularly women, we should wait for God to send us our mate. The Bible says take everything to God in prayer; the Father will send you the right mate at the right time. What we need to do is be patient and allow God to have His way in our life. After all, we are not put here for our will, but we are here for His good pleasure, to worship Him, to praise Him, and to be His mouthpiece in this world. However, what often happens is that our fleshly nature rears up and with our eyes we see a man who looks good on the outside (handsome), has a good job, and responds to our prompts. This type of meeting can steam roller into a sexual relationship very quickly, which shortly thereafter brings deep regret for one or both parties. Some of us have been alone so long, that the first decent looking guy that comes along who displays any interest, we take the ball and run with it without even taking a careful look at the situation that is being presented to us. Self-respect, as well as respect for the feelings of others, has fallen by the wayside. Sexual sins are on the top of the list for those who are in the world and those who are in Christ. There is a big old lust spirit that is loose in the church and instead of the saints standing up and taking authority over that demon, they are allowing Satan to get them all caught up in the fantasy of a relationship (which usually happens with someone else's husband).

Wake up saints! Rebuke and bind that demon and **CAST HIM OUT.** There are people in the church who are jumping out of one man's bed and into another's and then saying "Oh, I am the victim, have pity on me." You only hear this when the man dumps them or is mistreating them. The point of the matter is that for all of your sexual sins, whether fornication or adultery, you will incur the consequences of your lack of judgement. Not only will you bring curses upon yourself, but on your innocent children and grandchildren as well. Don't let Satan have his way with **YOUR OFFSPRING**. Take control of the situation, set a good example for your children. Discuss with them the problems that arise from teen sex and sex before marriage. Tell them what the Bible has to say. Remember that children most often do what they see at home. The effects of generation curses can be nullified; you don't have to suffer because of it. Make the change not only for yourself, but also for future generations. Accept Jesus Christ life and give the problem to Him.

Chapter 6

Dear Practitioner

I am turning on the spotlight. There is no use in running because you can't hide. I couldn't, neither will you be able to. First, I would like to establish a couple of points before I precede any further. I am not writing this chapter to mock or hurt anyone, nor to point my finger at anyone, I write to you out of love. I am writing you this letter because the Father, Almighty God, Jehovah Jireh has requested me too. He still loves you too, dear practitioner. He desires to have fellowship with you. It is out of His loving kindness that He is calling you to repentance. And there is another reason "Greater is He that is in me, than he that is in the world, and because I have the Christ living inside of me, I write to you out of love.

When God took the blinders off of my eyes, I could see that the enemy had been using me. It made me sick to know that I had been serving him. Now I sincerely want to make up for all the damage that was done by my hands. I thank God for His mercy.

I'm here to tell you that if you are not in agreement with what I am saying, if you do not feel convicted of leading others astray and for participating in these demonic practices, then I exhort you to go before God and plead for mercy. Ask Him to show you the truth.

Beg, pray and plead if you have to, that He will reveal the truth to you. Once God has shown you the truth, you then need to destroy all the tools that you have used as part of your rituals. Renounce Satan and all his devices. Get on your knees and confess before Almighty God, asking Him for forgiveness for every sin that you have committed. I know that this is easier said than done, but it must be done.

Fear will come into play here. You can be sure that Satan will try many kinds of tricks to stop you dead in your tracks. He will try to make you feel guilty for what you have done. He may tell you that God will never forgive you. But the devil is a liar because the Word of God says: *If we confess our sins, he is faithful and just and will forgive us our sins and purify us from all unrighteousness.* (1 John 1:9).

If you do not seek God on this issue and repent, you will suffer the ultimate consequences and your soul will be lost. Beloved, there is a place for Satan and all of his angels, it's called hell. If you do not repent and renounce Satan and all of his devices you will end up right there with him, which is exactly his plan. I know that many of you have taken people for their life savings, you have bought homes, cars, jewelry etc, off the blood and sweat of desperate people. You have participated in the masquerade.

How many times has someone needy come to you for "spiritual advice" and you told them that someone had put a "job" on them or to make it clearer, someone had put "roots" or witchcraft on them? Out of desperation, they believed your words. Then you proceeded to tell them that you could do "the work," even though it would take time, and it was dangerous because you would be fighting dark spirits. To make the work appear sincere, you prepared a bath for them to use as a spiritual weapon to combat the dark and evil spirits. Then you lower the boom on them: with supplies and your time, it would cost them $2000 dollars.

If it involved a mate, you would tell clients they would have to get their mate to take these baths, even if they had to trick them into it. You would suggest to them a way to get his participation, perhaps by running a nice bath for him after he comes home from a hard day's work. Now, I am not saying that many of you did not genuinely think that this person had witchcraft on them. Even if you really believed you could help this person, Satan has sent you a lie. He knows the deeper you get involved with his masquerade, the harder it will be for you to become free from it. Satan sends you an illusive vision or word. He will tell you some truths about a person to draw you both in even more. Usually the clients will go home and tell their family and friends and the lies disperse. This opens the door for Satan to get more captives. The fact is, outside of the freeing power of Jesus Christ, there is nothing that you can do to remedy that person's problems. There is only one problem maker (Satan) and only One problem solver and He is our Lord and Savior Jesus Christ.

I came under attack when I left these practices behind. I experienced sheer exhaustion and tiredness. It seems as though it took all that I had to get out of bed every morning. The clients stopped coming. The enemy tried to put doubt and fear into my head; sending practitioners to ask me why I left. And to remind me that I would be back. Watch out for fear and doubt, Satan's most powerful tools. (See chapter 9). Not only do I recommend that you give your life to Jesus Christ, but I also strongly suggest that you ask the Lord to cover you in His blood and seek out a Deliverance church. You will need to confess your sins to God, as well as others and seek true repentance. (See chapter 10)

I would also suggest that you read about deliverance. You can find good books in any Christian bookstore. Start going to church, and begin to fellowship with other Christians, filling yourself with the Word of God. Now I'm not going to kid you, the devil will be angry with you. As long as you stay under the Blood of Jesus Christ and follow in His footsteps, the Lord will protect you. The Lord said that he would rebuke the devourer for you. He also said: *That no weapon formed against you shall prosper.* (Isaiah 54:17). Put your faith in the Lord, Jesus Christ and praise Him for He is worthy.

Now there are those of you who are deceiving people with no remorse. You who have no scruples and are selfish. I don't have to name you, but you know who you are. You are just like your father, the devil, whom you willingly serve. Keep this in mind, whether you believe it or not, the Word of God is true. It is more powerful then any two-edged sword. Neither you nor your father can stand up against it. I rebuke you in the Name of Jesus, and I exhort you today to choose whom you are going to serve, whether it is Baal, or God. As for me and my house, we will serve the Lord. Oh! Glory, thank you Jesus. Remember if you continue in your deceiving and lying ways, your day is coming. If it is not now, it will be on Judgement Day.

Chapter 7

Who's That Spirit?

Human spirits are another area of interest for God's people that have brought many stumbling blocks into their lives as well as into their families. When I was growing up, my mother used to say that her deceased mother came to her to tell her about something, usually a warning of some sort. This is an old tale that many people still allow to reign in their lives. It is believed that human beings that formerly lived, go into the spirit world, and can bring back information. Some even believe there are earthbound spirits who neither went to Hell or Heaven but are stranded and caught here on earth because either they committed suicide or did not want to leave the earth realm. Although the Bible tells us that the dead know no more; *For the living know that they shall die: but the dead know not any thing, neither have they any more a reward; for the memory of them is forgotten.* (Ecclesiastes 9:5).

How do we explain how the mediums or even how the spirits of people who once lived appear to you in a dream? Well the answer is clear-cut, they don't. The simplicity of this will baffle many of you because you want to believe that old grandma Helen came to tell you to play this number, or to get rid of your boyfriend, or to accept someone new into your life. The fact of the matter

ck to the old deceiver we call Satan, who
id for more than six thousands years. He
out how human beings think; what attracts
th... it doesn't. Satan knows that human beings
are very inquisitive about the supernatural and desire to
communicate with deceased loved ones, angels or other
spiritual beings. So Satan has created various lies to
entrap you and take the focus away from the only One
who should have your full attention, and that is Almighty
God. So Satan has created the theory that you can speak
to deceased loved ones and other spirit beings. These are
the seducing spirits spoken about in 1 Timothy 4:1: *Now
the Spirit speaketh expressly, that in the latter times
some shall depart from the faith, giving heed to
seducing spirits, and doctrines of devils.*

However, there are times when God has sent angels
to deliver messages to His people; angels who have taken
on human form, but even when God sent His angels they
always testified and announced that they were sent from
the Father Almighty God. Angels from God will testify
that Jesus Christ is the Son of God and that He is Lord.
Other spirits, which are of Satan, will not. They will try
to deceive you by telling you some truth, so that they can
get you to rely on them, and eventually they will have
you involved in something that is sin and against the will
of God. Demonic spirits can take on the likeness of
family or friends to deceive you, and they also speak
through mediums. The Bible has this to say about it:
And no marvel; for Satan himself is transformed into

an angel of light. Therefore it is no great thing if his ministers also be transformed as the minister of righteousness; whose end shall be according to their works. (2 Corinthians 11:14-15).

Don't be fooled by spiritualists, mediums, channelers, and psychics who will tell you that they know the difference between a good spirit and bad spirit; they do not. There is only one way to be able to discern a spirit and that is through the gift of discernment and/or by what it confesses or tells you to do. The Bible says: *Beloved, believe not every spirit, but try the spirits whether they are of God; because many false prophets are gone out into the world. Hereby know ye the Spirit of God: Every spirit that confesseth that Jesus Christ is come in the flesh is of God.*

As children of an Almighty God, who is worthy of all of our love, trust and commitment, we could have better health, love, family life, supernatural power and protection if we would heed God 's Word, which is the Bible. If we would rely on God daily to give us our provisions, we would have a better quality of life.

The Psychic Network is a multi-million dollar telemarketing business. We are all familiar with telephone psychics. They have bombarded every household in America, claiming to offer truthful, spiritual advice to everyone who calls in. Each time you turn on your TV, there is an infomercial about psychics promising to supply you with all the answers for your life.

Thousands of people call these toll-free numbers

only to hear a recorded message that directs you to a 900 number with the promise of a live gifted psychic waiting for you on the other end of the call. Many times this number will cost from $1.99 to $3.99 per minute. The majority of the time the company will offer the first three to five minutes for free. This is the "hook-line-and-sinker" routine. They know that if they can just get you to call in for that first three minutes they will be able to hold your attention for the next 25-30 minutes.

When I first became aware of my gift of prophecy, I did not understand exactly what was happening to me. I had a woman suggest that I work for a psychic line. Since I knew that God had a plan for me, but it was unclear as to what it was exactly, I saw this as an opportunity to help people.

The first psychic line that I applied to mailed me an application, which I filled out. Sometime later a gentleman advised me that I would need to obtain a dedicated line in my home, so that whenever I was working, there would be no interruptions. No one was to be able to utilize that line; the purpose was to accept calls only for that psychic hotline.

He went on to instruct me on how to handle each caller. He told me that I should never predict death or illness. That I was to make sure that I kept the caller on the line for at least 20 minutes. He said first I was to tell them something that was true in their life, next, I was to do a general reading on them, which would take up at least the next 15-20 minutes or more. He never tested me, or verified to see if I had any gift. He was simply interested in the money that his organization would make. Let me shed some light on the misconception that psychics make a lot of money. When you work for a psychic line, you are only paid 25 to 35 cents per minute. There are usually no health benefits since they hire you as an independent contractor. Most people on the hotline do not care one way or the other about your problem. They will tell you whatever you desire to hear in order to keep you calling on a consistent basis. Most people are hooked after the first call. They are unscrupulous and will play on your desperation and weakness.

The Network has ministers who are working the lines. Now, I am not saying that the psychic lines do not have some individuals who are actually trying to help people, they are just using the wrong vehicle to do so. While working for the psychic lines, I talked to hundreds of people throughout the United States. I met people from all walks of life and most of them had one thing in common and that was that they were in a great deal of emotional pain. Many of the callers were extremely fearful of something that was happening in their lives. Most of the callers were women looking for Mr. Right, but kept finding Mr. Wrong.

I did not remain on the psychic line because whenever a caller phoned in, I would instruct them to get into prayer and to start calling on God's help, as well as other things. Also, I did not keep them on the line for long periods of time, so as results, my averages were low and this was brought to the attention of my employer. Not only did my employer not like my averages, but also I learned that they tape all conversations. So they knew exactly what I was telling the callers. My employer expressed his dislike for what I was doing, so I quit. Understand that the information psychics receive, no matter how accurate, is not from God. Satan is the main operator of these lines.

During the time I worked for these psychic lines, I realized most callers were poor, unsuspecting individuals. Callers would end up with whopping phone bills of $1000 or more. Worse yet, these people still were not getting real answers to their problems. Psychic lines are not concerned about their callers. Satan is the main operator of these hotlines. Whether you realize it or not, if you are working for a psychic hotline you are feeding into Satan's lies and he is using you to help destroy people. Do not be a party to his destructiveness.

Psychic Consultations

When you consult a psychic or medium (usually they are one and the same), know that you are seeking the advice of an evil spirit. It may appear to be the sweetest little old lady, or man, or an innocent young girl. No matter how sweet, gentle or kind they seem, the information they give is not from God; it is demonic. If you entertain this spirit, you open yourself up to all kinds of lies and deceptions. Demons will tell you certain truths to keep you coming back for more answers. This is the main function of psychic networks, which are daily making large sums of money from others' desperation. People who consult psychics have focused their attention away from God, lost faith in His infinite wisdom. And are unknowingly relying on demons for answers to their problems. These unsuspecting people have created more problems for themselves through their God-less search for answers. Satan has been condemned; he is on death row.

The One and True Living God has rejected him and now he wants God to reject you. Satan knows that you are the apple of God's eyes. The devil knows that God wants you to have a personal, loving relationship with Him. Satan knows that God wants you to totally trust in Him for everything you need. Satan is constantly trying to deceive you through psychics and mediums and crystal healers and other New Age nonsense.

Psychics have become the new psychologists of this decade. People often pay large amounts of money for a consultation with a psychic and/or medium. Most psychics will do whatever is necessary to keep you, once they have you as a client. If the psychic has access to a spirit being, it knows exactly what to tell the client so that he/she will come back and pay more and bring others.

I write to you to say that I have witnessed entire families come under demonic influence beginning with one individual that went to a psychic. She tells her family members about that psychic. Other family members also decide to visit. This is how the possession begins. Most psychics do not have a law of confidentiality; there is no law that governs them on this matter. Once they get involved with you and your family, chaos prevails. This is Satan's way of working. Those demons that are working through the psychic will feel bound to share things with each family member, things pertaining to other family members, and before they know it, a great division occurs within the family. Often it is beyond repair.

If you are considering attending one of the many seminars or lectures on how to develop your psychic abilities, or how to channel angelic beings, ponder this first. There are many people in the world who truly want to help people, and who with good intentions attend these classes and buy books pertaining to the New Age Arts. Once you start getting involved, you feel empowered. You feel as though you have embarked on a new journey that will bring enlighten-ment. This feeling of empowerment causes you to venture forth getting even deeper into the deceptive New Age practices.

You have entered into a spiritual realm of which you have no knowledge. As mere students, most of you will not have spiritual discernment, the ability to detect the presence of spirits. More than likely, you won't know it's there, what it is, or why it's there. This is a very dangerous position to be in. This may very well become the door by which a spirit enters into this realm and creates problems in your life, or the lives of others. You may be wondering what things spirits can do. Let me just name a few; depression, feelings of loneliness, eating disorders, sickness, lust, and anger leading to ultimate possession.

Yes, there are individuals who allow unknown spirits to possess them and speak through them. Entities that exist in the spirit realms are deceptive; they seek to make contact with human beings. Some of them will come with an illumination of light all around them, and they will speak to you and tell you their names, offer guidance and all levels of information to you. Most people who encounter these types of spirit beings are intrigued, thinking that these beings have chosen them to bring enlightenment to. This is where and how the entrapment starts. A spirit knows your weakness and it will use you to accomplish its desires here in this realm.

Beloved, there are only two spirits that exist in this world. Either it is the Spirit of the Lord, which is the Holy Spirit, who when He speaks to you will identify Himself and will attest to our Lord and Savior, Jesus Christ. The other is the spirit of Satan, who himself masquerades as a *angel of light* (2 Corinthians 11:14) (NIV). The Bible says that (Satan) the (thief) comes to steal, kill and destroy (John 10:10). Satan wants to deceive you by making you believe that you can become more spiritually enlightened and empowered through the use of tarot cards, developing your ESP or by communicating with angels.

The Bible says: *Every good gift and every perfect gift is from above, and cometh down from the Father of lights*. (James 1:17) Almighty God has given gifts to men for the strengthening, comforting and the edification of the church (the Body of Christ). These gifts are given to Christian so that they may evangelize the world. However, Satan has attempted to counterfeit and corrupt the things of Christ and has given his (Satan's) people certain powers of clairvoyance, clairaudience, divination, Reiki, transchanneling and past life regression, etc.

Praise God, that He is an Almighty God. The difference with God is when He gives us His Spirit it is the Holy Spirit, which is the third person of the Trinity. With Satan, the spirit that he sends to his messengers is a spirit of falsification. A lying, demonic spirit that will often disguise itself as a light spirit or a spirit of God. Satan wants to be like God and for this reason the Bible says (Isaiah 14:12-15, vs): *How art thou fallen from heaven, O Lucifer, son of the morning! how are thou cut down to the ground, which didst weaken the nations! For thou hast said in thine heart, I will ascend into heaven, I will exalt my throne above the stars of God: I will sit also upon the mount of the congregation, in the sides of the north: I will ascend above the heights of the clouds; I will be like the most High. Yet, thou shalt be brought down to hell, to the sides of the pit.*

Jesus Christ instructed His disciples to lay hands on the sick and in HIS NAME they would be healed (Mark

16:18). There are many that are advertising themselves to be prophets of God, not only in the secular world but also within the church. The Bible says: *But the prophet, which shall presume to speak a word in my name, which I have not commanded him to speak, or that shall speak in the name of other gods, even that prophet shall die. And if thou say in thine heart, How shall we know the word, which the Lord hath not spoken? When a prophet speaketh in the name of the Lord, if the thing follow not, nor come to pass, that is the thing which the Lord hath not spoken, but the prophet hath spoken it presumptuously: thou shalt not be afraid of him.* (Deuteronomy 18:20).

In the world today you have so called spiritual people using all kinds of titles. Be particularly aware, psychics are calling themselves prophets and healers. Some are even claiming to be coming in the Name of the Lord. Be careful, brethren and sisters, don't be fooled. If it does not lineup with the Word of God, DO NOT GET INVOLVED.

I was once tricked, deceived and God delivered me from the snares of Satan. My God, my Lord, He's my wonderful Counselor, my Deliverer, my Redeemer, my Strengthener, my Protector. Glory to His Precious Name. PRAISE HIM, for He is worthy to be praised.

The enemy knows that a house divided cannot stand. I ask that if anyone reading this message is involved in a situation like this, you should get on your knees before God and confess all of your past and present activities and ask forgiveness. Most importantly, STOP any contact with psychics immediately. (See chapter 9, Deliverance).

For those of you who use the Tarot, read the following.

During one of my counseling sessions, I met a young lady, Susan (fictious name). Upon Susan's arrival, the Holy Spirit directed me to ask her if she practiced New Age arts. With great enthusiasm, she responded "Oh, yes!" Susan practiced tarot card reading.

> *(Susan) "Tarot cards, are a tool that I use to have the ability to gain information about myself, as well as other people. Working with the symbols releases information from inside of my mind that I would not otherwise have. I cannot get the information without using the cards. I would like to be able to receive information without using the Tarot, but I do not know how to."*

Susan was not the only woman I have counseled who used the Tarot as an aid. Another individual I counseled intimated:

> *(Deana) "Whenever I use the Tarot cards, I believe that I am getting the answers that I need. However, my only problem is that I cannot figure out the time in the future when all of these situations will occur. I ask the cards if I am*

*going to meet a man. When I did the **Celtic cross spread**, which is in the shape of a cross with an extra set of cards next to it, I sometimes got two or three men in the future and outcome cards positions."*

Tarot Cards are another trick of the enemy. I have encountered people who believe tarot is an ancient art, dating back to Biblical times. This could not be further from the truth. The tarot is a tool of Satan. If you have tarot readings, just know that you are paying $100, on average, for information straight from demons.

When I first realized that I had a gift of wisdom, I met a lady who was a santera (a priestess in the religion of Santeria). She encouraged me to get a job where she worked. She worked for a very popular TV show, which has the readers on TV. When I interviewed with the show's employer, he informed me I would have to use tarot cards because the public needs something tangible to focus on. Although I told him that I did not use tarot cards, he insisted I use them. So I did.

My stay there was a very short one. In the months I worked there, I saw so-called *spiritual* people do horrible things to one another. People maligned one another and tried to cause others to lose their jobs. They used magic against each other. I was so unhappy with the atmosphere; I got headaches immediately after starting work each day. Whenever I was at work I would get a headache shortly after I arrived. I really disliked using the cards, one reason was because I had such difficulty

d another was because the other people in
the exception of two) were not actually
nation from the spirit world. They had the
definitions of each card printed right on the top of them.

Psychics who are able to access spirit beings are getting their information directly from *familiar spirits.* Familiars, also known as spirit guides, ascended masters, or light beings, latch onto you and give you information. Familiar spirits are usually acquired through psychic development, transchanneling, and certain kinds of meditation. Although the student is often unaware of the different types of spirits in the spirit realm, their desire for spirit communication leads to entrapment. Familiar spirits are demonic. They will offer very limited information to their victims to gain their confidence and influence their lives. If at anytime you decide that you do not want to communicate with these spirits, and ask them to go away, they will not leave. You will be unable to get rid of them merely at your command, for these are not spirits of God. They will infiltrate your thought patterns, give you conflicting information, and send you messages of fear until they are **cast out.**

I have encountered many horrific stories of demonic spirits who have entered the lives of students of the New Age. The demonic interference is directly related to the practice of New Age arts. One such story was a young woman who came to me for guidance on a situation that she was experiencing in her home. Her story follows.

Nancy (fictious name) as a part of her regular routine meditated every morning. She used meditation to "get centered," "to obtain light," and to receive guidance from what she referred to as her "spirit guides."

In the beginning everything seemed to be going wonderfully. She had visions of beautiful colors and beams of light. She said she met an Indian spirit, who said that he had been with her throughout her childhood. This spirit was very helpful to her at home. He would move things around in her house so that it was more accessible to her. If she misplaced some small object this spirit would relocate it for her. This was just some of the things he did for her. After awhile, Nancy decided that she no longer wanted to stay home. She was a freelance artist and she wanted to get a secular job. Here is where the problems arise. This spirit had become very attached to her. She had difficulty whenever she attempted to leave her home. If she decided she wanted to go out, she would begin to prepare herself. Then suddenly she would start to feel as though she did not want to go out or she would experience pain in a part of her body. At first she did not associate her problems with this spirit. As time went on, the situation got worse. She could not get out and go for a job interview. She couldn't get a job. Nancy had expressed a desire to have a mate but every time she met someone, for some reason (not always known to her) that person would disappear out of her life.

Nancy loved her artwork. She participated in exhibitions and had gained quite a reputation. However, as time went on she lost her desire to paint and as a result became greatly depressed. This is when she contacted me for a counseling session. During the time I was counseling her, the problems in her home accelerated.

Nancy's five-year-old grandson lived with her and began to have nightmares about a man who was continually bothering him in his sleep. Nancy, too, began to experience nightmares. She would dream of a man who would attempt to have sexual relations with her. He would show his penis to her and she would wake up screaming. As a result, Nancy began calling me at all hours of the night screaming and crying. She had become afraid to sleep at night. So she stayed up all-night and slept in the day. Eventually, the attacks began to occur whenever she would sleep, even in the daytime.

I then contacted other Christian minister friends and we began to pray about Nancy's situation. It was clear that this demonic spirit had taken over her life. Nancy needed deliverance from this demonic spirit. Although Nancy had grown up in a Christian home and was familiar with demonic spirits, she wasn't practicing Christianity. She instead had embraced the paganism of Native American tradition. Eventually, through our intervention, Nancy was delivered from this situation and her life returned to normal.

This is just one of the many horrifying testimonies that I have heard directly related to the practice of many New Age arts. If you are an individual who is experiencing strange situations in your life and you are practicing any of the New Age arts, I would strongly advise that you contact a Christian Deliverance ministry, or me, to get help immediately.

Satan wasn't always called Satan, his name was Lucifer. He was a very beautiful angel when he was in heaven. He had all kinds of crystals as part of his adornment (Ezekiel 28:13).

Now check this out! All you crystal wearers and healers, this was a part of Satan's attire, no wonder he is so familiar with them and still continues to utilize them now in his deception of God's people. If you go into any bookstore in the New Age section you will find a whole selection of crystal how-to-books. You will find crystal healing books, books on how to create mandalas out of crystals, wands, sacred portals and all kinds of things. These books were created to try to counterfeit the things of God. Satan, wants you to think that you can lay some type of crystal upon a person's body and heal them. The Bible says (referring to Jesus) *that we are healed by His stripes* (Isaiah 53:5).

Crystals are another popular tool that many are utilizing today. Crystals are beautiful stones to look at. There are many different types of crystals. Amethyst, quartz, jade, agates, carnelian just to name a few. There are all kinds of literature on how to utilize crystals in healing rituals, developing psychic ability, and strengthening your aura, etc. Some teach that you can enhance your entire vibrational field by working on the Chakras, energy fields located in spiritual bodies. People spend thousands of dollars on crystals to use them in these ways. Again, this is a deception, a masquerade that Satan has conjured up. This is still another type of counterfeit healing, which he has devised. In the Bible, Jesus said: *Go ye into all the world, and preach the gospel to every creature. He that believeth and is baptized shall be saved; but he that believeth not shall be damned. And these signs shall follow them that believe; In my name shall they cast out devils; they shall speak with new tongues; They shall take up serpents; and if they drink any deadly thing, it shall not hurt them; they shall lay hands on the sick, and they shall recover.* (Mark 16: 15-18).

This is the Great Commission that Jesus gave all of us, especially those who are born again believers (Christians). The healing power of the indwelling Holy Spirit (which as born again believers we received as a deposit at our conversion) shows us that all other types of healing are counterfeit and are not of God. Crystal healing, or Reiki healing and any other healing methods that are not done in the name of Jesus Christ are counterfeits. Satan uses his power to take away an individual's ailment, but this is just part of a deception that will eventually lead to a deeper involvement and link with him.

Chapter 8

My Testimony

Writing this portion of the book is not an easy task for me because it requires that I really take a look at what and where, I have been. I am sharing my personal experiences with you at the request of my Father, the One and True God. Also because I want you to receive your deliverance and to give your life to God. Although I will share with you many things, there will be things that I have left out because of the involvement of other people.

I had relocated to Pennsylvania in the earlier part of the year. I moved because of a man who I met while he was visiting New York during the Christmas holidays. During his stay here, we started to get know each other and he invited me to visit him in Pennsylvania for a weekend. Soon thereafter I moved in with him and we started to build a relationship. I was so enthusiastic about this relationship that the first thing I did was look for a job there. I got a job with an organization called Help Counseling, Inc. where I worked as a residential program worker. Afterwards, I got another job with the Veterans Administration, at a psychiatric hospital in Coatesville, PA. During this time I was on cloud nine. We had started talking about marriage after he promised to marry me. In the winter of 1991, I started attending Second Baptist church, where I was baptized. It was there that the Lord started to guide my heart. I decided that I wanted to teach Sunday school and was looking forward to it, until one day my so-called financé decided that he wanted me to leave and go back to New York City to my own apartment. We broke up in church. I had spoken to the pastor about my problems with my financé and he called him in individually for a counseling session and then we both came in to see him together. It seemed as though they had set this up the night before. My finance said that he wanted me to go. I had a nine-month-old baby by my finance at that time and so it was very devastating to me to have to leave.

I was so depressed when I left, just me and my baby, returning to NYC where my other two children were living with their fathers. Within two weeks, I could no longer bear it, and I had to send my son back to Pennsylvania. I was an emotional wreck; so much so that I would not even do my hair. I let myself go to a certain degree. I had low self-esteem and all I wanted to know was if this man and me were going to get back together again. All I could do is cry out to the Lord and for two months that's all I did. It got so bad that my friends did not even want to see me coming because all I could talk about was this man.

One night I was crying out to the Lord and I stretched my arms out to Him. When I did, a Light came around my arm, a bright light. I became afraid but in the next second or two, a voice spoke to me, a voice that was very comforting. The voice said, "You will have another chance."

At first, I thought perhaps, I had cracked up, but then I rationalized I had not, because now I felt a sense of peace flowing through me. I remember smiling. Although I did not know what happen. I felt safe. The first thing that I noticed in my bedroom was that there was no light, I was in total darkness, there was no light coming in from the window. So what was it? Well I wouldn't find that out for sometime.

A couple of days later, I was in the rent office of the development where I lived and I overheard a neighbor of mine talking about a couple who was able to tell people about the future. I went to this couple and they did not charge me, but told me a lot of things that were going on in my life pertaining to my ex-finance and other areas. All these things were true, so I was overwhelmed with what the lady and her husband were saying.

The husband went on to tell me that I was given a gift by God, a gift that enabled me to see things and to know things about people. He also said that I would help thousands of people. It was through my desperation that I even came to these people. I have reasoned with myself that these people were psychics because I did not believe in them but when the husband told me that something had recently happen to me in my home and I had a gift, I naturally thought what he was saying came from the Lord. Then he told me that he was going to help me develop my gift; he told me to buy a red candle and a Seven African Powers candle, which I could purchase at the grocery store. I went home and thought about it, then I did it. I set up an altar with a glass of water, a crucifix and a white cloth, just the way he specified. I burned candles to different saints on this altar as he told me to. I made different herbal solutions that came from a store called a botancia, which is a store that sells religious item such as catholic saints, herbs, and witchcraft things. I never did anything to harm anyone because I did not believe in that and because I believe that was of the devil and that God would punish people who did that. What I did not know is that Satan had set me up to fall. He knew that God had a calling upon my life and that I had a gift but Satan wanted me to use it to glorify him, instead.

Even though I talked about the Lord Jesus Christ and talked about Salvation, I was what the Word calls a double minded person. Although I loved the Lord, I was living in sin. Not only was I practicing idolatry, an abomination to the Lord. I was participating in witchcraft and leading God 's people astray. Now, when I think of what I did, it makes me sick. I am so sorry for what I have done. I have confessed my sins and have repented for them.

Satan used me for his kingdom; he literally tried to destroy me. I got involved with a religion called santeria, which is the worship of saints. I did what is referred to as "spiritual work" for people and got paid for it. I really thought that I was helping people, and I always prayed.

I was offered a job in a place where I would be on television and do readings for people on a psychic hotline.

Even though I did not refer to myself as a psychic, I realize in hindsight that was what I was doing. I continued to work in this area. Eventually, I got my own television show where people could call in live, and I would answer their questions. I would always tell them to stay in prayer and I would tell them that they needed to be born again and to accept Jesus Christ as their Lord and Savior. I even read from the Word of God, teaching people to rely on God, but at the same time accepting payment to help people. Satan really had deceived me.

I met a man who was a born again Christian, a preacher, and an ordained minister who knew the Lord. This man had received a Word from the Lord and the Lord told him that I had a gift but that I was in error. When he told me, I immediately wanted to find out how to change, because I knew that something wasn't right but couldn't put my finger on in. It was my consistent prayer before the Lord that if I was not serving Him in the manner which He desired me to, for Him to reveal it to me. I was willing to change because I knew that the Lord had a work for me to do. I also knew that the Lord had called me to be a minister. Apparently, Satan knew it, too, and continued to throw obstacles in my way.

However, God is Good and He sent people to help me get out of bondage. The preacher helped me in the Word and shortly after, I started working with him. He told me about a deliverance church that had a heavy anointing. I went to that church because I wanted to be delivered from all of the idols and demons, and the fear of getting rid of them. God delivered me out of the hands of Satan and brought me into His glorious kingdom. I threw all my statues into the river. I cast out all the demons from my house with the Word and got rid of all the stuff that was associated with them. Not only did God deliver me, but also blessed me with many blessings. I am so happy that I am free. I love the Lord and am willing to do whatever He wants me to do. I belong to Almighty God. The Lord revealed to me who I am in Christ. My sisters and brothers in Christ, that is why it is so important to wait on the Lord for everything. I got caught up into this by going to the wrong people, who told me that I had a gift from God. They could not tell me what God wanted me to do, because they were not of God, they were of Satan. I was involved in this for two years before I was delivered. To this date, it has been two years since and my life has changed completely for the better. I bless the Name of the Lord for His Mercy and ever Loving-Kindness. He showed me that I have a gift of prophecy and that He gave it to me for the glorification of His Kingdom. I cannot tell you all of the people who God has healed through me as well as using me to give them a word of comfort, exhortation and love.

Praise Him, and give Him all the glory. Instead of singing those worldly songs lift up your voice and minister to your Father. Bless His Name with a song of praise. Sing a hymn or a psalm of praise.

Chapter 9

Deliverance

Deliverance is a subject that it seems is both misunderstood and taken lightly by Christians and non-Christians alike. It's a subject that has made many people sigh and take a step or two backward. People usually shy away from this subject due either to fear or disbelief. The Bible says that we were "spiritually dead" in our trespasses, that we needed a Savior. Without Him we are doomed. The price paid at Calvary brought many things for us. Jesus' death wiped our "sin account" clean. Paid it in full. I am sure many of you are familiar with that term. Isn't it wonderful when you are in debt, and when you make that last payment, you receive a notice stating paid in full. What a feeling of relief.

Well, on a spiritual level that is what Jesus' death did for us, with one stipulation: that we believe in Him, ask Him to come into our lifes and change it, so that He will work out His perfect will through us. The Bible states that Jesus is our deliverer. Spiritual bondage is yet another reason why we need deliverance. As stated earlier, Satan comes for three reasons, "to steal, kill and destroy." When there is demonic activity in your life, there will be all kinds of interference. Some of you may say, "Well how does this come about?" Let's start by saying that there are only two spirits in the world. The

Spirit of the Lord, which is God Himself, or the spirit of Satan which comes either in the form of demons or Satan himself. Some of you may think that there are other spirit forms such as spirit guides or angelic beings that bring you daily guidance. But remember as discussed earlier those are demonic spirits in disguise.

Almighty God is a loving God. He is the One who gives us prosperity, health, abundance, success, happiness and all the good things in life. He loved you enough to create you and blessed you with good things. As stated earlier, it is at His Word that your body is healed from all illnesses. He draws close to you, He embraces and hugs you. He desires that you get to know Him on a 'personal level.' He wants a personal relationship unlike any relationship you will ever have, a trusting and committed relationship. When we form this type of relationship and bond with Him, the blessings will pour in. If you want to experience power and have supernatural experiences, then He's the Man for you.

The other spirit of which we spoke, is the spirit of Satan, who is unloving, cold, deceiving, monstrous and a liar. Satan will deceive you into believing that his way is the best way. Remember that God loves us and wants us to be close to Him, and because Satan knows this he purposely wants to ruin our lives. He wants us to lose fellowship with the One true God. When we get involved in his activities we create an opening for him to bring demonic interfere into our lives. Let me show you the many ways in which Satan seeps into your life.

Demonic oppression is often overlooked in people's lives. Whether you are a born again believer or not, you can be demonically oppressed. Many of us have unknowingly been oppressed at different times in our lives. Although demonic oppression comes in many forms, I will provide you with a few examples. Experiences such as serious health issues. I am not taking about when your body starts to breakdown due to the age factor. I am talking about when you start to get ailments for no apparent reason. Illness does not come from God, it comes from Satan. This is oppression. Another form of oppression is financial problems, even when you handle your finances. If you are having problems making ends meet, you can bet that Satan has his ugly hands in it.

Satan will operate in your thought-process. He will put thoughts into your mind of insecurity, anger, selfishness, lust, greed etc. Ladies who are in relation-ships, can identify with how Satan will bring thoughts of infidelity with reference to their mates. When you start to have the thought that your mate is seeing another woman without proof, so that you continually accuse your mate of having another woman, know that Satan is the influence. It is his job to keep you in despair, depressed, unhappy, sick and bombarded with feeling of low self-esteem. You must recognize that God would never suggest these kinds of things to you. He is a God of Love. Satan, on the other hand, will make these negative suggestions. He is extremely dangerous, evil and should not to be taken lightly or played with.

My Christian bothers and sisters, Satan can oppress you and will do so, if you do not take a stand and bind the enemy's interference in your life. As Christians and children of an all-powerful God, Jesus gave us the authority and all the power over the enemy. We can stomp on him (Satan) and make him give back to us, what he has taken from us. The authority comes from and through, Jesus Christ, the Lord of our lives. He gave this authority only to the Body of Christ, which is composed of all born again believers. For those of you who are not in Christ, there are steps that need to be taken before you can be set free. I will discuss that a little later in this chapter.

The next area of satanic influence I would like to discuss is demonic possession. Demonic possession occurs when a demon has taken up residence inside of you and has taken over your life. He talks for you, thinks for you and you have very limited, if any, control over your thoughts and feelings. You find yourself doing things and not remembering that you did them. Especially, things that you would never even conceive of doing. Your thoughts seem, for the most part, to always be negative and destructive. Confusion is very prevalent in your life. Demonic possession is the culprit. I am sure that many of you are familiar with the word 'exorcism.' When demons need to be exorcised, deliverance is desperately needed. Demonic activity can be needed in a lot of areas of your life, but one particular area is mental illness. Demons seek to take total control of your mind. There are many people who are in institutions for the mentally ill whose only problem is demonic possession. A demonic spirit most often plagues people who hear voices. I have encountered persons with mental illness who are demon possessed.

One story involves a time when I worked at a psychiatric hospital. I encountered a patient who was demon possessed. I will share his story with you.

Ron (fictious name) had been institutionalized since he was seventeen years old. At age forty-three, he displayed the behavior of a fifteen-year-old. Ron was experiencing what is called in the medical profession "grandiose delusions." He had three personalities and at any given time, one or another identity would surface. In one identity, he believed that he was God, and would refer to himself as God. If you referred to him by his real name, he would become crazed. Another identity he displayed was Satan. He would claim to be Satan himself and refuse to answer to any name, except that name. Occasionally he would snap back into reality and accept that he was Ron. He would be calm, but this state would last for only a short period. While I worked on the psychiatric ward, Ron displayed all types of behavior. He had sexual relationships with the some of the other geriatric patients, mainly homosexual. Even though Ron was not homosexual in nature, the demon within him would have him engaging in all kinds of acts. Another type of strange behavior that Ron displayed was the desire to drink rubbing alcohol. At times, with the doctor's permission, Ron would get a day-pass to go off the hospital grounds. When his day pass was over he would rarely return to the psychiatric ward. Two of the staff members would usually have to go out and search for him. Ron was usually found in the graveyard lying on a grave. These were typical demonic behaviors for Ron.

In a conversation I had with Ron, I asked him how he got this way. He said, "By using all kinds of hallucinogenic drugs such as LSD, uppers, downers, heroin as well as other drugs." Ron regretted using these drugs and strongly warned me not to use them. Through further analysis of Ron's mental illness, I discovered that Ron had significant involvement in the occult, which opened him up for demonic possession. Demons will often disguise themselves in activities such as drug use, as was the case with Ron. Although all cases of mental illness are not demonic in nature, through intensive research many have found that a large percentage of people suffering from mental illness are under demonic possession (Remember, all sickness comes from Satan). Ron is a good example of demonic possession. And, there are many others.

There have been people in mental institutions or on psychotropic drugs that have been delivered from the demons that were plaguing them. There are documented case studies of people who were delivered from demons. Once they were delivered, they returned to society to live normal, productive lives. If you know of anyone who is displaying these types of mannerisms, whether it is oppression or possession, suggest to them that demonic activity may be involved. If you are considering deliverance for yourself, know that a serious matter such as this requires action on your part. Once you recognize and desire to be delivered it will not be easy. Becoming entangled with demons is easy, but being set free is not. It takes commitment, acceptance, faith, obedience and courage. It takes a total change in lifestyle. You will never be the same again. You change for the better if you live by the rules set before you.

I would like to establish a couple of things before we get into what deliverance requires. First of all, no one can perform a deliverance ceremony unless he is in Christ. Which means a born again Christian who is walking according to the Word of God. There are different New Age practitioners, as well as other religions that claim to be able to get rid of demonic spirits. This is absolutely unfounded and untrue. The Bible says: *And when they were come to the multitude, there came to him a certain man, kneeling down to him, and saying. Lord, have mercy on my son: for he is lunatic, and sore vexed: for oftentimes he falleth into the fire, and oft into the water. And I brought him to thy disciples, and they could not cure him. Then Jesus answered and said, O faithless and perverse generation, how long shall I be with you? how long shall I suffer you? bring him hither to me. And Jesus rebuked the devil; and he departed out of him: and the child was cured from that very hour. Then came the disciples to Jesus apart, and said, Why could not we cast him out? And Jesus said unto them, Because of your unbelief; for verily I say unto you, If ye have faith as a grain of mustard seed, ye shall say unto this mountain, Remove hence to yonder place; and is shall remove; and nothing shall be impossible unto you. Howbeit this kind goeth not out but by prayer and fasting.* (Matthew 17:14-20).

Every disciple of the Lord has been given this authority. Jesus commissioned us: *Go ye into all the world, and preach the gospel to every creature. He that believeth and is baptized shall be saved; but he that believeth not shall be damned. And these signs shall follow them that believe; In my name shall they cast out devils; they shall speak with new tongues; They shall take up serpents an if they drink any deadly thing, it shall not hurt them; they shall lay hands on the sick, and they shall recover.* (Mark 16: 15-18). This is the "Great Commission" that Jesus ordered us to fulfill. You must be a born again believer to be able to take authority over Satan and his demons. As a born again believer you have the Spirit of the Living God in you. It is through His name and by Him that demons are cast out. Don't be deceived, do not let people tell you that if you pay money to any of these New Age practitioners, they will get rid of your demons. This is false and propagated by Satan and his followers.

Seeking deliverance should be done prayerfully. You

100

must first submit yourself to God and renounce Satan and all of his activities. Next, you need to accept Jesus Christ as your Lord and Savior and ask Him to come into your life. If you have difficulty doing this, seek out a Christian Church that believes in deliverance, that is, a full gospel church.

Speak with a minister, tell him your problems and ask him to pray with you about the situation. Deliverance teams have been established in some churches. Most often these are people who have accepted a calling to be part of a deliverance team. Once a minister or the head authoritative person in the church has determined the need for deliverance, deliverance counseling should proceed.

In deliverance counseling the minister will explain all the areas. And what is needed before deliverance can be attempted. Let's make it clear to those of you who are considering deliverance. One of the most important things that should be done before the deliverance ceremony, if at all possible, is that you realize your need for a Deliverer and that you accept Jesus Christ as your Lord and Savior. You must be willing to receive His salvation. Jesus is the One who will deliver you from the snares of Satan, without Him you are doomed.

There is a very good, important reason why you should be born again. When the demons are exorcised, or cast out, they will attempt to return. Jesus said: ***When the unclean spirit is gone out of a man, he walketh through dry places, seeking rest; and finding none, he*** *saith, I will return unto my house whence I came out. And when he cometh, he findeth it swept and garnished. Then goeth he, and taketh to him seven other spirits more wicked than himself; and they enter in, and dwell there: and the last state of that man is worse than the first"* (Luke 11:24-25) For this reason, it is very important that you have the Holy Spirit living inside you.

Remember two spirits cannot live in the same body. Once Christ is there, Satan cannot take up residence again. The Holy Spirit will heal you of everything that Satan brought upon you.

God did not create His people to live in bondage. The Word of God says *For God sent not his Son into the world to condemn the world; but that the world through him might be saved. He that believeth on him is not condemned: but he that believeth not is condemned already, because he hath not believed in the name of the only begotten Son of God.* (John 3:17-18)

If you decide that you want to receive Jesus Christ in your life. This is the Word of God that you need to apply to your life. *That if thou shalt confess with thy mouth the Lord Jesus, and shalt believe in thine heart that God hath raised him from the dead, thou shalt be* <u>*saved.*</u> *For with the heart man believeth unto righteousness; and with the mouth confession is made unto salvation.* (Romans 10:9-10)

I have encountered Christians and non-Christians alike who do not believe that deliverance is necessary.

Jesus Himself went about healing, teaching and casting out demons. He stated that this would part of the ministry of born again believers. He empowers us so that in His Name we can help set free those who are captives of Satan. For your edification I will share an account of deliverance that occurred with a student of mine in March 1999.

My students and I were at a miracle healing service when the prophet called for those who were in need of prayer, whether for sickness, finanical problems, etc. My student, Erica, went up to the altar and when he asked her what she needed prayer for, she said, "Depression." The prophet laid his hands on her and began to speak to that "spirit of depression." To her surprise, as well as others, Erica began to scream and screech as though she was in pain. The more she screamed, the more intensely the congregation prayed. What we were witnessing was a demonic "spirit of depression" being cast out in the Name of Jesus. Erica was saved before this encounter, but when she was delivered from "depression," there was an immediate change in her voice, which was stronger and more confident. She had dark circles under her eyes that literally disappered overnight and now she is full of joy. Erica's story is just one of many. We praise and glorify God for His power, love and protection.

7/15/07

Became prostrate before God to get in the position to receive your promises

Chapter 10

The Blood

Blood is a substance that we all have in our bodies. Medical science confirms that humans cannot exist without blood. It carries cells, water, vitamins, minerals and sometimes germs. Two of the major life destroying illnesses of our time are Leukemia (cancer of the blood) and HIV (AIDS).

We have white blood cells and red blood cells. Blood takes in oxygen and travels through every organ in the body. These cells play a major role in our lives and without them we would die. The Bible says that the blood carries the personality. In this society people take all kinds of herbal blood cleansers, such as Golden Seal. However, there are times when these cells and herbal cleansers will be of no help in the physical or in the spiritual. Although we are all familiar with blood, how many of us are familiar with the Blood of Jesus Christ? What is its purpose and what does it mean for us? There are old hymnals about the Blood; Christians talk about the Blood. What is so special about the Blood of Jesus Christ? Jesus Christ shed His Blood at Calvary's cross for you and me the Bible says: *and without shedding of blood is no remission.* (Hebrews 9:22)

Satan knows how blood can play an important part

in a sacrifice. In practices of idolatry, blood sacrifice is practiced. In the religion of Santeria there are many rituals that incorporate the blood of doves, pigeons and others animals. It is believed that certain orishas or gods (some consider them to be angelic beings) require certain blood offerings that are included in drinks and other solutions. The idea behind the blood offering is to appease the orishas of choice and thereby receive their good favors. The practitioners ask their favorite orishas to bring them love, happiness, luck and prosperity, etc. There are many other pagan religions that embrace the same blood sacrifices. The brotherhood of Satan also utilizes blood in many of their ceremonies.

The blood element brings about the power that they desire and want. All pagan religions, including Santeria, belong to Satan. He uses different names but they are all doing his work and are directly paying homage to him. Any religion that does not acknowledge the Father, the Son and the Holy Spirit, and does not serve the Almighty Father through His precious Son Jesus Christ, is devil worship - satanic. Satan has disguised himself in these religions, particularly the New Age. In the Old Testament, God the Father dwelt with His people of Israel in the Ark of the Covenant. In the temple there were two tabernacles: the first tabernacle the priests went into to accomplish the service for God. The second tabernacle, which was called the Holiest of All, only the high priest was allowed to go in with the blood sacrifice, which he offered for his, and the people's sins. Jesus

came and died on Calvary's cross offe[...]
for our sins by the shedding of His Bl[...]
says: *Neither by the blood of goats and*
his own blood he entered in once into th[...],
having obtained eternal redemption for u[...] or if the
blood of bulls and of goats, and the ashes of an heifer
sprinkling the unclean, santifieth to the purifying of the
flesh; How much more shall the blood of Christ, who
through the eternal Spirit offer himself without spot to
God, purge your conscience from dead works to serve
the living God? And for this cause he is the mediator
of the New Testament, that by means of death, for the
redemption of the transgressions that were under the
first testament, they which are called might receive the
promise of eternal inheritance. (Hebrews 9:12-15)

If we know that the Blood of Jesus sanctifies us, why would we choose to participate in ceremonies with the blood of goats, bulls, chickens or any other animals. Jesus died and gave His Blood as a once and for all offering. Anyone or anything that requires you to bring offerings of blood is demonic and is of Satan. If you are participating in practices right now and you have to offer up blood, be it an animal's or your own, I exhort you to cease practicing it. Renounce Satan, confess your sins before God and ask for forgiveness and accept Jesus Christ as your Lord and Savior. At that moment your sins will be wiped clean you will have a new life in Christ.

I don't know about you, but this makes me want to get on top of the roof and shout out His holy and precious Name. As God's people, we are too precious to give our treasures away to Satan or anyone else. God said: *Before I formed thee in the belly I knew thee....* (Jeremiah 1:5). Which means before God made us, He knew exactly who we were and what He wanted us to do. It is our responsibility to find out what special job He has planned for us to do. What special gifts He has ordained us to have, and most of all, what special treasures He has locked up inside of us. It is no secret God loves us; that's why He made us.

I know this, and even the devil knows it. If you don't understand it, then you need to pick up the Word of God and read it for yourself. Don't let Satan continue to steal your blessings. Jesus' blood is powerful and once you are under the blood, it will continuously cleanse and protect you from Satan's harm. There are so many wonderful blessings once you are saved. Not only will you gain ETERNAL life but also will be sanctified, justified, and co-heirs with Christ. God has so many blessings in store for His people; they are too numerous for me to name, but just to give you an idea read Deuteronomy 28:1-13 in the Word of God.

Christ and I want to invite you now to be a part of His glorious kingdom, a kingdom of abundance, prosperity and most of all, of love. What we could not do ourselves, the Blood of Jesus Christ, the Son of Most High God, did for us.

Forgiveness is one of the most misunderstood words in the English language. Most of us feel that we know exactly what forgiveness is, but experience has shown me that most often people do not know what forgiveness really is. The human definition of forgiveness, as to what it is, where it comes from and how we go about receiving it is still puzzling to many. How do we embark on forgiveness, this entity we know so little about? All of us may have partaken of Forgiveness many times throughout our lives. When you were a child and a friend did something to you and it hurt, you would go through the pain of it all, but then forgiveness comes to pay you a visit and you forgive and become friends again. Forgiveness can have her way with you, because in this stage of development you are very receptive to her.

As we reach adolescence, our perception of what people do to us changes. We begin to hold grudges that hinder us in many ways. Although God the Father wants and sends Forgiveness to our door, we often do not hear her knock, or just won't let her in. Many of us say that we forgive, when we actually hold resentment and bitterness toward others about whatever caused the hurt in the first place. Trusting people is easy at first, but after a few brushes with deception, your trust begins to fade away and suddenly it becomes hard to trust anyone. So many walls are built up because of the inability to forgive. The Bible speaks a great deal about forgiveness. In the Lord's prayer in Luke 11:4 Jesus says, *And forgive us our sins; for we also forgive every one that is indebted to us.*

There are other versions of that same prayer, but

forgiveness still plays the same role. Forgiveness is the reason why Jesus died on the cross, in order that we could be forgiven of all our sins through the appropriation of His death.

Remember that you are a blessed, beloved child of God. No matter how far astray you have gone, there is redemption through Jesus Christ. Seek Him and you shall find. Walk on His path because it is the only way to true joy. Peace be with you all.

If you would like to contact the author:

Rev. Diana Hardy
2124 Broadway, Suite 389
New York, NY 10023

Website: *www.livinginthespirit.org*

Impac **t** *ian*
Chris **Books**

332 Leffingwell Ave., Suite 101
Kirkwood, MO 63122

AVAILABLE AT YOUR LOCAL BOOKSTORE, OR YOU MAY ORDER DIRECTLY. Toll-Free, order-line only M/C, DISC, or VISA 1-800-451-2708.

Write for *FREE* Catalog.